MASS
INFLUENCE
The Habits of the Highly Influential

Teresa de Grosbois
with Karen Rowe

Cover image and design by Bilal Fayyaz

Text copyright © 2015 by Teresa de Grosbois and Wildfire Workshops Inc.
All rights reserved.
First Hardcover Printing, 2015
First Paperback Printing 2015
First Ebook Publication 2015
Canadian Cataloguing in Publication Data
de Grosbois, Teresa M., 1964 –
 Mass Influence – The Habits of the Highly Influential
ISBN: 978-1-926643-10-6 (Trade)
ISBN: 978-1-926643-11-3 (Hardcopy)
ISBN: 978-1-926643-12-0 (e-book / Kindle)
I. Rowe, Karen, 1975 –
II. Title

Shameless self-promotion
Here's what people are saying about
Mass Influence: The habits of the highly influential

"*Mass Influence* is an engaging, easy read. Whether you're out to change your company, your community or your industry, this step-by-step guide will support you in becoming an influential thought-leader."

Marci Shimoff, *New York Times* bestselling author *of Happy fo No Reason* and *Chicken Soup for the Woman's Soul*

"Someone said, 'It's not what you know but who you know that really makes the difference.' Wise words indeed. Teresa de Grosbois makes a compelling case in this excellent book about the value of influence. Easy to read, eminently practical and loaded with important exercises, this is the perfect road map for anyone who desires to become a significant person of influence."

Les Hewitt, *New York Times* bestselling author of *The Power of Focus*

"A valuable resource for anyone passionate about influencing positive change in the world. If you are prepared to lean into a bigger impact, you'll want to read this book."

Barnet Bain, producer *What Dreams May Come* and *The Celestine Prophecy*; author *The Book of Doing and Being*

"If you loved Malcolm Gladwell's *The Tipping Point*, *Mass Influence* is a must read. Influence expert Teresa de Grosbois masterfully deconstructs the time-immortal strategies of influence and guides you to massively impact the trajectory of your business and your life."

Steve Olsher, *New York Times* bestselling author of *What Is Your WHAT? Discover the ONE Amazing Thing You Were Born to Do*

"Influence is not something that just happens—it's something you can learn to do. Learn from the best! Teresa de Grosbois will guide you to grow your business through becoming massively influential. Oh, and you'll have fun in the process!"

Ellen Rogin, *New York Times* bestselling author of *Picture Your Prosperity*

"This book is a game-changer. Teresa's forward thinking is eye-opening and mind-blowing. If you're an entrepreneur, business owner or leader, this book is a step-by-step blueprint for establishing yourself as an authority in your industry. After you read—and more importantly apply—the simple habits in *Mass Influence*, you will never go back to your old way of thinking or operating. Teresa makes it easy to become influential and build influential relationships."

Charmaine Hammond, international bestselling author of *On Toby's Terms*

"At the beginning of the book *Mass Influence,* Teresa de Grosbois confesses that she has 'created some epic failures' in her life. This book is not one of them! You will discover the obstacles stopping you from becoming an influencer. This book helped me to recognize how to become influential— and made it so clear, interesting and easy to understand. We all desire sway, impact and positive power: Mass Influence is the guidebook to get you there. Highly recommended!"

Debbi Dachinger, international bestselling author and award-winning syndicated radio host

"A must-read for every business leader! This book blows away misperceptions of influence. It is sure to inspire you and give you access to unlimited possibilities. It's easy to dip in and out of and it is full of bite-sized wisdom on giving influence and growing your own influence. It brilliantly lays out common mistakes to avoid and the expertly-designed exercises assist you to up level your own influence."

Lisa Mininni, bestselling author and president, Excellerate Associates

"Such a needed book, Teresa. I'll be sharing it with all our coaches and trainers. It's like an 'agent of change' how-to manual. So excited to spread the word."

Jennifer Hough, international author, speaker, and founder of Get Out of Your Own Way

"When it comes to influence and connecting, there in no one in the world who does it better! Teresa is an absolute expert and will demonstrate how to grow your business extremely quickly by following simple rules. This will become your go-to book on taking all relationships and connections to unprecedented levels of success."

Colin Sprake, international bestselling author of
Entrepreneur Success Recipe and owner of Make your Mark Training

"Teresa de Grosbois is my 'influencer' role model as well as a role model to my colleagues in the world of transformational leadership. Being a hub of influence, generously connecting individuals for their mutual benefit and elegantly self-promoting seem as natural to Teresa as breathing. Yet in this book you'll discover that these are skills anyone can learn and thus expand our reach, our success and our impact on the world. Thank you, Teresa, for once again exhibiting your generosity by sharing your powerful secrets with us all."

Debra Poneman, bestselling author, founder of Yes to Success, Inc.
and co-founder Your Year of Miracles, LLC

"Read this book. But before you do, set aside everything you think you already know about how to become influential and grow your business through influential relationships. De Grosbois lays out the how-to steps of becoming highly influential like you've never seen before. It's fun, entertaining and will change the way you think about networking in business."

Lesley Everett, Founder and CEO Walking TALL International,
president of The Global Speakers Federation 2013-14

"It's not every day that a book like this comes along. Run, don't walk to get this book if you want to grow your influence, your business and your reach in the world. It's fun, entertaining and life-changing."

Dr. Lin Morel, bestselling author of
Soul Lifts: From Bumps to Brilliance

"This book is easy to read and it's easy to absorb all of Teresa's amazing information with real action items that anyone can immediately implement. Pick a copy up and don't put it down!"
Tonya Hofmann, CEO and founder of The Public Speakers Association

"If you desire to create change in the world, to tap into the power one person can leverage through 'mass influence,' this book will give you the rules, the tools, and most importantly, the mindset, to have you win at the influence game on a large, even world-changing, scale."
Julie Ann Turner, bestselling author of *Genesis of Genius* and host of the Global ConsciousSHIFT Show

To Shawne, who helps me fly,
to Pam who grounds me, and
to Rae and Fiona, who teach me joy.

Acknowledgements

I am a billionaire in my friends.

Karen Rowe, you are a rock star of a writer and I could not have done this book without you. Pam Bayne, you have helped with every step of the process and, without you, the book would still be a pile of blog posts and half-formed thoughts

John Demartini, your willingness to invest in other people's leadership inspires me. Thanks for your investment in me.

To my test readers and coaches, I love you. You simply rock: Randy Peyser, Ella Chesterman, Neil Thrussell, Marilyn Suttle, Charmaine Hammond, Justin Robinson, Tina Thrussell, Jaden Sterling, Frank Moffatt, Prab Lashar, and especially Jill Fischer and Alicia Dattner for helping me find my sense of humor.

Randy Gage, you are a gift to the speaking profession, not only in what you teach but in how you create the space for all of us to become better. I am blessed to have you in my court.

And most importantly, Shawne Duperon—you make everything I do better. I simply love you.

Contents

PREFACE 1

INTRODUCTION 3

PART 1—NEW REALITY, NEW RULES 9

Chapter 1: The Mindset of Influence for the Good of the Many 11
    Stepping into the Influence Game 13
    The World is Your Free Agent 16
    The Reason You're Here 18

Chapter 2: The Unspoken Rulebook 19
    Bragging vs. Shameless Self Promotion 26
    Self-Promotion and Influence 29
    Influence vs. Fame 30

Chapter 3: Understanding Wildfire 33
    Spark 34
    Fuel 37
    Wind 41

PART 2—THE HABITS OF INFLUENTIAL PEOPLE 45

Chapter 4: Here's the Overview You're Looking for 47
    The 10 Habits of Highly Influential People 48

Chapter 5: What's Your Problem? 51
    Habit #1: Playing Big 52

Chapter 6: Are You for Real? 67
  Habit #2: Authenticity 67

Chapter 7: Speaking to a Crowd 79
  Habit #3: One-To-Many 79

Chapter 8: Show Me the Money: Influence as a Currency 91
  Habit #4: Influence as a Currency 91

Chapter 9: Your Relationship Capital 95
  Habit #5: Building Powerful Relationships with Other Influencers ... 95

Chapter 10: Understanding Cycles of Reciprocity 111
  Habit #6: Creating Cycles of Reciprocity 111

Chapter 11: Connecting the Connectors 121
  Habit #7: Connecting the Connectors 121

Chapter 12: The Hub 125
  Habit #8: Become a Hub for Other Influencers 125

Chapter 13: Rock 'n' Enrollment 133
  Habit #9: Influencers Are Masters at Engaging and
  Enrolling Others 133

Chapter 14: Taking Action, Living Your Dreams 139
  Habit #10: Influencers Take Action 142

Resources and What's Next 147

About the Authors 149
References & Definitions.. 15 1

Preface

Understanding Mass Influence

Mass Influence draws mostly on my personal observations and teaching. Although the ideas delve into a new realm, I'd like to acknowledge some brilliant thinkers who have influenced my work.

Broad-scale (or mass) influence is distinct from individual influence. Individual influence, which was studied by Robert Cialdini in his book *Influence: The Psychology of Influence*[1] is the ability of one person to influence another. I recommend it, although many of the principles of one-on-one influence change when you move into the realm of mass influence—the ability of one person to influence large groups of people.

The subject of books like Malcolm Gladwell's *The Tipping Point*[2] or Chip and Dan Heath's *Made to Stick*[3], is the influence of one individual on the masses. Even before reading these great works, I knew I wanted to dive deeper into the influence conversation to get more practical, real-time information on becoming influential. In my conversations with colleagues and clients, I found I was not alone. Many others shared their stories with me of blindly having ineffective conversations with gatekeepers[4]. When I got the tools to effectively befriend the gatekeepers and build relationships with the influential, my world opened up. I'm excited to pay that forward. *Mass Influence* picks up where the ideas of other books leave off by giving you the rules, the etiquette, the mistakes to avoid and, most importantly, the mindset of how to win at the Influence Game.

Introduction

I have created some epic failures in my life.

Most of them start in my mind.

The first failure I remember happened when I was two, just starting to speak.

I am sitting in the corner of a crowded kitchen, jostling for space along with my nine siblings and a dog. Everyone is in a rush to finish something or get somewhere. I, the youngest, sit unnoticed in my corner. My overworked, exhausted mother has forgotten to feed me. I watch her scrape food into the garbage.

I'm angry. Pissed off, as only a two-year old can be. I cry in frustration.

"I'm not important." I tell myself. "I'm less than the stinking garbage."

I accept the thought as true.

That inner dialogue sticks with me.

It does not matter that I grow up in a supportive, loving family, or that my mother and I become close as adults and she becomes one of my greatest role models. "I'm not important" runs in the background of everything I say and do. It is both the driver that helps me succeed and the trap that has me fail. This inner mantra has both caused me to make my life about becoming a force for change in the world and has motivated me to say some of the stupidest things that could ever escape my lips.

The Influence of Inner Dialogue

Everyone is writing about inner dialogue these days. What many authors fail to point out is that while your inner dialogue is inescapable and humiliating, once you're able to see it for what it is—a story that you made up based often on one isolated incident—it's also hilarious and wonderful. Befriending your inner dialogue that you created when you were a child and using it to motivate you rather than destroy you is the foundation for your success in the Influence Game.

Learning the Influence Game, like any other game starts with understanding the strategies and rules. One of the most important tools you can develop is to learn about and understand the concept of broad-scale or mass influence.

What Led to *Mass Influence*

I first became intrigued with studying and mastering the concepts of influence because I didn't have any. As someone with the inner dialogue of "I'm not important. I'm worth less than the stinking garbage," I was spending the bulk of my time doing one of two things:

> 1. Looking for evidence to validate that I wasn't important (ask my former husband how many times I falsely accused him of not making me a priority); or
>
> 2. Looking for ways to become important through career or business choices.

Observing the behaviors of influential people and learning from those who had influence became a passion of mine.

Everyone wants to have influence in one way or another, but are you clear about what you want specifically, or what influence means to you? Influence could mean more power or more money. Maybe you want to be flown around in a private jet, be friends with Oprah, or even become Oprah. Maybe you are frustrated by something in the world, and want to change it. You want to start a movement and create long-lasting change.

The entrepreneurial world is full of examples of people who started

IF GANDHI HAD NO PERSONAL POWER

small, whose passion and ability to inspire the imagination of others resulted in attention and energy flowing towards them.

Mass Influence embraces a simple idea: what makes Steve Jobs Steve Jobs or Martin Luther King Jr. Martin Luther King Jr.?

Most people think it's somebody else's job to create change. Consider that it's your job. You are the leader you've been waiting for and in order to be that person, influence is crucial because it helps you create change—from a small scale to massive shifts on the planet. The influential path enables you to take action, to motivate others, to spread the word, to create a movement, to be your own Bill Gates or Mahatma Gandhi.

So, what will it take for you to play at a bigger level?

My own desire to create change in the world became truly real for me just after the turn of the millennium.

I'm sitting on my living room floor, eyes closed, attempting to clear my thoughts. I am just coming out of a really bad year. My father has passed away, my health is failing, my business has failed, and to cap it all off, my marriage has ended.

I'm feeling annoyed at the world. My life sucks. There is a litany

5

of complaints in my head. "Why doesn't somebody fix ... my life, the broken sidewalk in front of my townhouse, the world."

I breathe deeply and my mind finally settles. A crystal clear thought emerges.

"I am somebody!"

I resist the thought. "These are not my problems," my mind insists.

"I'm somebody" my mind repeats.

"It's not the world's job to fix my life. My job is to improve the world."

My heart stops. I weep.

In that moment I know, without a doubt, that like so many others, I am the one the world is waiting for. And I can either live a life of complaint, or a life of action to create a better world.

I choose action. My life changes.

How often have you thought, "Why doesn't somebody just...?" Perhaps you wish you could change something in the world. But how do you actually step into having enough influence to "be the change you wish to see in the world"? Every college dorm in North America has the famous Gandhi phrase posted on the wall, between a class schedule and a poster of an indie band.

What is required to actually be the change?

Enter the Influence Game.

Most people don't understand the principles of how to play the Influence Game to become an influential person. It's like you're standing on the rink in the middle of a hockey game and

you've only ever been taught how to play badminton. Understandably, you don't know why all these people are shooting pucks past you and skating around you on the rink.

You will discover in this book the three obstacles that are in your way of being taken seriously as an influencer, and exercises to transcend those challenges:

1. What you were taught as a kid

2. The habits you created when you first learned to network in business

3. What your inner voice tells you in moments of deep discomfort.

Whether it's change within your community, your corporation or the world at large, the principles of mass influence are the same. By the time you reach the final page of this book, you will have ingrained, at a habitual level, a solid understanding of the game and how it's played. You are invited to work on developing routine habits that will continue to build your fame and influence. The exercises are designed to help you integrate influence into your thinking and routine. Most importantly, you'll be able to look at where your inner game is having you fail.

Mastering the concept of what creates influence can be a hard idea to grasp, much less follow. Yet, like riding a bike, once you master being influential, you'll wonder how you ever thought it was hard.

PART 1
NEW REALITY, NEW RULES

You make a living by what you get, but you make a
life by what you give.
–Winston Churchill

CHAPTER 1

The Mindset of Influence for the Good of the Many

"Never doubt that a small group of thoughtful, committed citizens can change the world; indeed, it's the only thing that ever has."
—Margaret Mead

Next time you're curled up with a latte and your computer, ready to pull something up on Netflix, watch *How to Marry a Millionaire* from 1953 with Marilyn Monroe and Betty Grable. Feel free to fast forward. The story line is predictable. It's reflective of a dominant theme you see in the 1950s—don't judge people for "shallow" reasons. Three girls decide to marry rich. Amidst their antics, they fall in love with three seemingly ordinary guys. One of them turns out to be really rich. All of them live happily ever after, without any bearing to how much money their men have.

I love watching movies from the 1950s. Not because they're particularly good, but because they're such a stark benchmark of where society was a half-dozen decades ago. Watch a movie from the 1950s or even the 1990s and you'll gain a clear sense of just how rapidly the dominant thinking of society is evolving. The dominant themes of this movie—the idea of judging a person based on wealth or the notion that a woman would need a man to gain wealth—are now antiquated.

Movies are a great benchmark for how rapidly society is evolving.

There's a massive shift in global consciousness going on. The shift is happening on two levels.

First, people are waking up. They are learning to use their whole brains and to master some of the higher brain functions such as intuition and empathy. It is no longer uncommon in business to hear the term *whole brain*.

Second, people are tuning into the power of relationships, and the level to which we are all connected on this planet. The opinions of the masses are moving far more rapidly than the political systems can keep up with.

The rapid change in popular opinion and belief systems is largely due to the second level of shift in consciousness: a massive shift in the flow of information. The old model of people working for corporations is shifting into a new paradigm of people becoming information workers.

When Henry Ford's moving assembly line became wildly successful, he doubled wages to pay his workers $5 a day in 1914. Thousands of prospective workers arrived at the Ford Motor Company in Detroit drawn by this salary increase. Today, the flood of people seeking to find work looks different. Now we can produce information, rather than just physical goods for big business and individuals can work from home for some of the largest companies in the world[5].

People, whose primary product or service is in the information realm, now work online in fields such as information gathering or development, training and education. The opportunity now exists to change global thinking around certain conversations, planet-wide, far more rapidly than ever before. Arianna Huffington had a varied and interesting career in media and politics, but the creation of the *Huffington Post* launched her to a different level of influence. As a blog and news aggregation site, the *Huffington Post* has more than a million readers comment each month—an online empire with real-time evidence of a highly engaged community[6].

Those changes are happening whether or not you're a part of them.

They are happening at every level, from broad-reaching international initiatives to local communities, to changes within a single organization.

To facilitate these changes, people want to be led by someone who inspires them, who is out for the good of the many, who will step up and into their own influence for the good of the group, and the good of the planet.

What will be your role in this massive shift of global consciousness?

You can either be a leader in that change or you can be a follower.

To be influential you must be willing to become a leader.

Stepping into the Influence Game

Today is one of the best times in history to move into the Influence Game. Gone are the days where a few outlets governed when and how everyone received their media. Many no longer even watch the traditional news or read national newspapers. Instead, they're finding out about major world events from Twitter and Facebook. The world has become your free agent, and anyone, even you, can become an overnight success, or "go viral" in ways that we never dreamed of in the past.

The Influence Game still runs on the same principles it did prior to the emergence of the Information Age. Mass influence comes from developing relationship with numerous people. But the ease with which you can do so is far greater now than it was a couple decades ago.

Back then, the Internet was really just starting, and the ability to grow a following online was in its infancy. To hold significant influence was a long, slow process and developing your own tools of influence was very challenging.

For instance, 20 years ago you "became famous" by developing relationships with reporters and journalists or becoming a newspaper reporter or journalist yourself. You might have become a politician or perhaps a church minister. Options included radio host, professional speaker, writer or columnist, starting a magazine or becoming a book reviewer for a journal. You could have started a charity or a training company to teach a specific skill. Whatever the case, you would have then had to seek out people in person. You might have called up book reviewers or found an agent or publicist who had the connections in the industry to properly promote your field of expertise.

Opportunities were limited and not readily accessible. The average person working a 9-to-5 job would have had difficulty finding a way to break into developing that kind of influence. If you weren't in one of these positions, or connected to people who were, your ability to develop your own tools of influence was a great deal more challenging. Mass influence was unattainable for the average person.

Being Your Own Agent

In today's world, the Internet and social media have brought about the opportunity to spread ideas, products and concepts instantaneously. You can develop your own tools of influence with ease and, within a short period of time, quickly develop a platform to launch your dream. It's as easy as developing a following on Facebook, an online radio show (known commonly as a podcast) or a personal blog. Anyone can become influential—the technology is available to all of us. We've moved into an era where "game changing" is accessible to everyone. There is simply a set of habits and skills to be learned and adopted.

You now have the ability to become your own agent. When you think about how the idea of influence has changed in the last two decades, the evolution is almost mind-blowing. The traditional realms of influence are still there, but we've layered on a whole new level that didn't exist 20 years ago.

At the same time, there is a set of rules and habits to game changing. Just as if your dream is to play in the NBA, you would start with learning the game of basketball, to play the game of influencing change, you start with learning the habits and skills of influencers.

The challenge? It is not common to see influence as a game with a set of rules or a skill set you can learn. Some people believe that if they are really good at what they do, the world will beat a path to their door.

"Oprah would interview me if she met me," Janice's passion jumps through the phone.

Janice is a first-time self-help author and I'm coaching her on the skills and strategies needed to put a book on the bestseller lists. She's emphatic that she does not need to learn to be intentional about becoming influential.

"My work is that good," Janice says. I believe her. She is not arrogant. It's the calm knowing of someone who delivers a high contribution to others.

"I know," I say. "I've read your work. But what makes you stand out from the thousands of other people who do really great work and want to get noticed by Oprah?"

Janice stops. The conversation is at an impasse. Both of us believe that there is something the other does not see. She is not wrong. There is something to be said for doing exquisite work that is of high value to the world. Sometimes, exquisite work alone is enough to bring you that amazing break.

"I believe in flowing with what's in front of me," she says. "What I need tends to just show up."

I point out that what has showed up is me—someone who teaches the skills of developing influence and we laugh. "If you had a child who was a virtuoso piano player, would you say, 'He does not need piano lessons!' Or would you find someone amazing to teach him the skill at the highest level?" I ask.

She understands the point and we move forward to create a plan for her to build her own influence.

The World is Your Free Agent

It's June 22, 2013, and I am inordinately relieved. I am watching CNN. It's been an exhausting week and I am close to tears from the pressure. Calgary, the city where I live, has suffered one of the worst floods we have ever seen in Canadian history. No amount of sandbags or flood control measures are working. All efforts have been in vain.

Our entire downtown core is under water. More than 100,000 families are displaced. One-third of the city is without electricity. Traffic has ground to a halt as most of the bridges are closed from damage. Miraculously, in a city of over a million people, only four people are dead. Stories from around the city of heroism from rescue workers fly across Facebook and Twitter.

A Facebook photo of my daughter's school shocks me. Water is half-way up the main doors. It's one of the oldest schools in the city and many of the city's archival photos are stored in the basement. Much history has been lost.

Like most of my neighbors, I'm exhausted. I've been helping friends rescue their homes and dealing with water issues on my own property. Since my property is on high ground, the damage, fortunately, is minimal. I know I'm lucky, but somehow, I'm taking it personally that our flood is not being covered in the U.S. news. In my own thoughts I've made it important that Americans know what's going on. When terrorists attacked the twin towers on September 11, 2001, or when Hurricane Katrina devastated New Orleans in 2005, our Canadian cities sent members of our fire departments down to help. Now, tired, exhausted and frustrated, I'm wondering where our U.S. neighbors are.

In the midst of my self-pity party, something interesting happens. The Calgary flood, or rather the hashtag #CalgaryFlood, trends on Twitter. It becomes one of the top hashtags being posted. CNN notices and suddenly our flood is being covered in U.S. news.

The next day we hear the White House has phoned our mayor to see if help is needed.

I laugh at the irony. I have stewed for seven days wondering when our U.S. neighbors would notice. I teach people that we are the media. Yet somehow, hip deep in water helping a friend save her house, I have forgotten what I teach.

The simple truth is this: our American neighbors didn't know. My brooding over the situation did not change a thing. My picking up the phone and calling CNN or sending them an email with a few photos of what's going on with a plea for help could have made a difference.

My thinking that the United States should "just notice us" is not unlike Janice believing that Oprah should just notice her. I have an unspoken rulebook too, and the rules in my head trip me up as easily as the next person. Like a lot of women, I've even been known to do this on a date, thinking the guy should just *know* Princess Teresa's guidebook for a fun date.

We're human. We create beliefs all over the place that don't really serve us.

It's become almost cliché in business, the notion that "we are the media." Have you ever thought about what that really means, that you can pick up the phone and call the media and what you post on the Internet matters? Yet in a world demanding rapid information,

the first broadcasts when a tsunami hits Japan or a hurricane hits New Orleans are typically on Facebook, Twitter and YouTube and you, with your smart phone or tablet, have become one of the frontline reporters.

The Reason You Are Here

You may have a bigger vision for your life or your business or maybe you have a higher purpose and want to make your life count for something. Yet are you spending all your time answering email, or dealing with clients one-on-one, mired in the muck, so to speak? When you're stuck in the muck, you can't really create the traction you want to move to the next level.

One of my joys in life is helping thought leaders use influence and fame appropriately so they can have more impact shifting our global culture into a more positive mindset. Influence and fame are just tools, but they are extremely useful tools. Whether you want to serve your organization or the planet as a whole (the two aren't really that different), you can use mass influence in your leadership to create shift. You can be a world changer.

One of the first concepts to understand is that anyone can create a community and a conversation around themselves. Learn how to connect your community to other communities and other conversations that are similar to yours and you can create a movement. Occupy New York, Stop Kony and Project Forgive, for example, are three grassroots movements begun by individuals who used the Internet and social and traditional media to create communities and conversations which connected with other communities and conversations. The connections went viral, blossoming into worldwide phenomena with far-reaching impacts.

Once you understand the Influence Game, and learn its skills, the changes you want to see become yours for the creating. The following pages show you how to take advantage of this new flow of information to spread the message you want the world to hear.

CHAPTER 2
The Unspoken Rulebook

"You have to learn the rules of the game. And then you have to play better than anyone else."

—Albert Einstein

Merit Alone Won't Get You There

Becoming more influential isn't about more money or more promotions. Playing the Influence Game is about understanding that top influencers play by an unspoken rulebook. Money and promotions often follow. But understanding the rulebook comes first.

You are born, or ingrained, with a rulebook that you subconsciously apply to most situations in your everyday, adult life. Think of Robert Fulghum's wildly popular New York Times bestselling book, *All I Really Need to Know I Learned in Kindergarten*. The hard truth is, sometimes the rulebook you followed and the ideas you were taught as a kid—such as "share everything" and

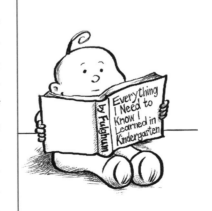

"play fair"—work against your ability to create change and be effective in today's business world.

Unknowingly, you may believe that if you're really, really good, you shouldn't have to point out your merit to other people. If you have written the best book on the planet, or you have developed the best system to help people succeed in business, the world should just notice. It's true that merit is a major part of the equation for true influence. Yet merit alone won't take you there. There is a skill set to learn.

Chances are you have beliefs that you don't even know are there, beliefs that are affecting your ability to influence. One of the ideas I invite you to consider is that what you've been taught as a kid, or what you may have learned when you first learned to network in business, are actually the habits or beliefs that are in the way of you being taken seriously as an influencer.

Just like Janice, who believed that "Oprah would interview me if she knew me," I see these beliefs in myself as much as I see them in others.

I see my own limiting beliefs one day as I digest an email from a potential member of the Evolutionary Business Council (EBC). The EBC is a collaborative organization of which I'm the founder, bringing leaders of vision together to expand global change.

The potential member is referring to a phone call on which Dr. Stephen Hobbs, owner of the WELLth Learning Network[7], requested support.

Let me set some context.

Steve Hobbs changed my life.

It's late 1999 and I'm in the audience at one of Steve's events. He's talking about the concepts in his book Living your Great Life *and we're doing an exercise around who we would be if we knew we could be anything. I'm deeply uncomfortable. The idea is causing me to really look at my job. I'm a leader and I like what I do. But I can't say I love it. The excitement of my life doesn't get me out of bed in the morning. It's not what I would have dreamed of doing as a child.*

The realization is a catalytic moment for me. I know, without a shadow of a doubt, that I am meant to leave my corporate job and start my own business.

Twelve years later Steve and I still have a deep mutual respect for one another. I credit my start as a speaker and writer, not to mention a good share of my success in business, to this man. I feel blessed to call him a mentor and friend. Likewise, as one of the founding members of the EBC, he has contributed to many members' dreams in a similar fashion.

The EBC connects people. It's what the EBC is based on. We create deep relationships with people we respect and admire and then connect them with others who are liked-minded. Many members of the EBC have this level of respect and relationship with Steve and with each other.

The potential member has recently been on one of the organization's collaboration calls, where Steve has requested testimonials for his upcoming book, Help Them Help YOU Manage-Lead. *I join the other members on the call in responding with an enthusiastic "hell, yes!" Having participated in Steve's workshops and been a colleague of his for more than a decade, I know the quality of his work, the depth of his commitment to leadership, the level of his expertise. I know his relationship to integrity, to contribution and to excellence.*

My respect for Steve is so great I support him unequivocally and without hesitation. The unspoken rule being that if something he's doing isn't a fit, or doesn't resonate, I can bow out. I have the choice of saying yes or no at any time and I know that Steve, or any other member, will not take it personally.

In this same moment, the potential member sees that we EBC members said yes without first reading Steve's book. For him it lacks integrity. He's now emailing the entire membership, questioning the integrity of our organization.

I am at first shocked to see this showing up because I'm dealing with a successful businessman. Then it hits me: he doesn't think it's fair! He is emailing us with a complaint stemming from his unspoken rulebook. He doesn't like that testimonials are being requested. His unspoken rule is, if the book truly has merit, people should just offer their praise. He also doesn't like that people say "yes" before reading the book.

He misunderstands what our organization does, our mission, what it's about, and most importantly, a very foundational pillar of the organization, which is the strength and depth of our relationships in business and in life. I realize, also, that he fundamentally misunderstands the rules of the Influence Game.

He has shown up on the rink in the last three minutes of the final period. He doesn't know what went on in the game before he got there. The foundational problem is I've failed to give him a true sense of what's going on in the game. More importantly my own belief of "the etiquette and rules should be obvious to him" is also in the way.

There are now unspoken rules being broken. Emailing that many influencers at once over a minor issue that could be resolved by picking up the phone is creating commotion in the organization. Emailing might have been appropriate in certain circumstances, but not in an organization of influencers.

I'm realizing, with embarrassment, the primary failure is mine. I put a player on the rink who has no idea of the rules of the game he's stepping into and is not at all related to the other players.

Simply put, relationship marketing as a practice recognizes the long-term value of relationships as a basis for referrals, testimonials and support of any kind.

How many times has this happened to you: a close friend asks if you'd like to do something Thursday night, and you say yes before knowing

Pop Quiz: How ready are you for the Influence Game?

Which of the following beliefs is true for you?

☐ I should not have to tell others about my work, they should notice.

☐ I should not ask others to endorse me.

☐ I think endorsing others is a nice gesture, but I typically don't do it unless I'm approached.

☐ If someone offers to endorse me, it would be wrong for me to suggest what they say.

☐ The next time I meet an influential person, I should offer to buy them a coffee.

☐ Social media is a waste of time.

☐ People just use social media to sell themselves.

All of the above are possible limiting beliefs. While they could be effective in some circumstances (e.g., it can be very appropriate to buy a colleague a coffee), they may limit your ability to build influential relationships in a high-influence situation. To effectively play the Influence Game, re-wire them by focusing on the opposite positive action or belief.

the plan. You love and trust your friend, and you want to spend time together; it doesn't really matter what you're doing because you know you'll have fun. Influential endorsement often works on that same level of trust.

In other words, if I've been doing business with you for years, or have a deep sense of relatedness to who you are, what you're about and how your business runs, I will not hesitate to offer to endorse your book because I know, like and trust you. I already know your content, I have a sense of what your book will be about, I know you're a great writer for the audience you serve and I can confidently know I will love the book. So I'm happy to say "yes" and then later read the book. That's a high level of trust, and that's what relationship marketing and the Influence Game is all about.

Working with my students, I discovered that many people have ingrained the reasonable idea that if you do really great work, the world should notice and beat a path to your door. As a result, you may carry a big list of "shouldn'ts" around in your back pocket, such as:

- *"I shouldn't have to seek influential relationships in business."*
- *"I shouldn't have to promote myself—that's cheating."*
- *"I shouldn't have to tell someone what I'd like them to say about me or my work because it's not authentic. They should just 'know' what to say, and they should take the time to write the testimonial themselves."*

All of these *"shouldn'ts"* are based on a belief that selling yourself is wrong or bad or dirty. Consider that these beliefs can keep you two steps behind, no matter how hard you try to move forward. Consider that they are actually "shoulds" that, when done authentically, will contribute to your success. You could:

- Seek influential relationships in business
- Promote yourself
- Tell people what you want them to say about you and your business.

Authenticity and Purpose

"Efforts and courage are not enough without purpose and direction."

—John F. Kennedy, Jr.

When you're naturally in the flow of your purpose, the fame and

24

influence will come as soon as you put the actions in place that garner fame and create influence. Influence requires you to take your place among the community of influential. And true influence stems from keeping your focus on serving others.

Do Exercise 1 and think about the area in which you want to hold influence. Do you want to be influential in the area you work or do you want to be influential in your passion? What endeavor do you most love? If you're really lucky, your work and your passion are one and the same. If not, you're going to have to choose what focus you're working to hold influence in.

My students often tell me they have vastly underestimated the importance of this exercise early on in their learning of the Influence Game. Having a vision and knowing where you want to get to allows you

Exercise 1: Where Do You Wish to Hold Influence?

Note: The exercises in this book are downloadable from the 30 Day Influence Challenge, which is a bonus program included with this book at www.MassInfluenceTheBook.com

1. Decide the area or topic in which you wish to hold influence. The area may be one or all of the following:

   - Aligned with your work or business
   - Something with which you've personally been challenged
   - Aligned with a personal passion, such as the environment, business, education, health

Now consider what problem you would solve for the world and for whom you would solve it (e.g., Problems—Shortage of water, how to effectively manage change, literacy, arthritis. Audiences—Dry-land farmers, entrepreneurs, students in low-income neighborhoods, elderly).

to measure your progress as you move through these exercises.

You're going to be revisiting this question after you do additional exercises in this chapter. If you're struggling, just guess for now and come back and rework your answer later.

Think of this exercise as if you're trying on coats; you have to try on a few before you know what coat you truly want to wear. Sometimes you may even buy the coat and keep it for years, simply because it's close to what you want, but you're not sure where that perfect coat is. For now just put on a coat. Pretend we're looking in a mirror together and you might say things like "the arms are too long" or "it's the wrong color."

In the same way, you're going to try on a brand. What area are you keen to hold influence in, what problem do you solve and for whom?

In trying your coat on, you're going to see parts you don't like and parts you really want to keep. But you won't see that until it's off the rack. Just grab a coat, any coat you think might be close, and let's start.

Bragging vs. Shameless Self Promotion

"Our deepest fear is not that we are inadequate. Our deepest fear is that we are powerful beyond measure. It is our light, not our darkness that most frightens us..."

—Marianne Williamson

*"A lot of us have shame around self-promotion and mistake it with its pushy cousin, **bragging**."*

—Shawne Duperon

When you read the phrase "shameless self-promotion," what comes to mind for you: that stereotype of a greasy, inauthentic salesman, or a self-confident, helpful, passionate and talented individual who can help solve your problem?

The phrase "shameless self-promotion" can sometimes have a negative connotation. What would it be like to *not feel shame* when you share how you can assist others? Freeing? Powerful? Transcending shame is the foundation of personal power.

Another way of saying shameless self-promotion is by "owning and speaking your unique reason for being on the planet" to others with clarity and passion and *without* holding back.

How do you distinguish the difference between bragging and shameless self-promotion? It's all in how you say it.

Emmy-award-winner Shawne Duperon is an expert in gossip and teaches the distinction between the two: bragging is a push; shameless self-promotion is a pull.

"It doesn't really matter what you're saying; it's about how you're saying it. Bragging is all about you. Shameless self-promotion is all about you with confidence.

When you're in that bragging realm, it's narcissistic, while shameless self-promotion is confident. When you're bragging, chances are you're in desperation mode. In contrast, when you're shamelessly self-promoting, you're in a deep love mode. When you deeply love what you're doing, and you know the difference you can make, you will naturally talk about it because it would be a crime not to. When you come from that place, miracles start to manifest.

When you're really good at shameless self-promotion, you don't even need to open your mouth. Your way of being is confident and clear so that people naturally attract to you, especially those of influence.

Try saying "Can I brag?"

A great example is when you say to your four-year old niece 'You're so pretty,' and the four-year-old replies in her sweet, innocent and endearing voice, 'Yes, I am.' It's that place of being that is so lovely and so honest, where shameless self-promotion is authentic.

It's innocent and pure—versus when you ask a 16-year-old, who is ornery and annoyed, and their response is, 'Yeah, whatever.'

Who you are being is more important than what you're saying. When you're in desperation, you're in lack. And when you're in lack, you can start feeling like you're in that bragging energy. Bragging is inauthentic, and people can feel it and pick up on it quickly. It simply doesn't work."

Consider your dog or cat's energy when they invite you to play. Your dog jumps up and down. The cat looks at you like you're a bit dense until you get what her pressing a paw against your arm means. In both cases their energy is self-confident and magnetic. The dog is not bragging about how fast she can get the ball. She is simply running to invite you into the game.

When you stay in the mindset of being of service to others, you are on the love verses fear side of the spectrum. You stand in the realm of what you might call "love of your fellow man." That's a completely different context than, "I don't like to brag", "I need to brag about myself to be famous and influential" or "I need to brag about myself to bolster my self-worth."

If you truly want to be of service to others, there may appropriately be a part of you that wants to be famous because you want your work to make a bigger impact. With fame and influence comes the ability to help more people. This type of desire for influence can be useful to yourself and others.

However, when your primary goal in life is to be famous, you're barking up the wrong tree. If your motivation is to have a lot of people love you, your inner dialogue is desperate and you come across as bragging. When your motivation is to tell people about your work so you can help them, your inner voice is saying the same thing as your outer voice. You're authentic.

Self-Promotion and Influence

Just as there is a difference between shameless self-promotion and bragging, there is also a difference between self-promoting and influence. Imagine a continuum, where bragging would be on one extreme end, self-promotion is in the middle and influence is at the other end.

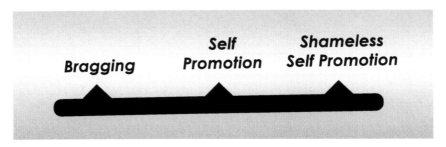

To move into influence, you need to have the self-confidence to be able to shamelessly self-promote because you are impassioned by who you are. The key is to understand that it's not your self-promotion that makes you famous or influential. That's not the path to influence, but this step is foundational. This distinction is somewhat of a paradox.

Within the paradox, the key point to understand is that shameless self-promotion can't make you influential, but an inability to talk about yourself with self-confidence or shame will stop you from becoming influential. If you're not confident enough to assist others by demonstrating who you are, what your credentials are, and how you can help them, you won't have other influential people feeling confident in talking about you in the same way.

Influencers naturally seek to help each other. A good hockey player will naturally prefer to pass the puck to a teammate whom they're confident will know what to do with it when they receive it. Likewise an influential person is more confident making connections for you or endorsing you if they know you know the game.

Step one: when speaking with other influencers make sure they know what problem you solve for other people.

Exercise 2: Introduce Yourself with Intention

For the next 24 hours, change how you introduce yourself to the following format:

I [solve what problem] for [what group of people].

Notice any difference in the way people respond to you and write it down.

Influence vs. Fame

Which would you prefer—influence or fame? You may not have considered the question before, but understanding the difference will allow you to win effectively at the Influence Game.

Fame is when many people know you. Influence is when many know, like and trust you. Fame would be Kim Kardashian or Miley Cyrus. Influence would be Oprah Winfrey or Nelson Mandela.

It's not enough just to have many followers who know of you; it's about reaching that level where others know what you stand for, like you and will easily take recommendations from you.

Stop for a moment and think what a recommendation from one highly influential person would be worth to you. Think about what an endorsement could mean for you in the context of what opportunities you are seeking right now that might easily come to you.

Your answers to Exercise 3 will vary depending on how big you can

Exercise 3: Estimate the Value of an Endorsement

Name three influential people whose endorsement could make a significant difference to your career or business.

1. _____

2. _____

3. _____

Estimate, if they endorsed you, how many more people would know of your work? _____

Estimate what their endorsement of you would do for you financially

a) In new opportunities ($/year) _____

b) In increased sales ($/year) _____

c) In cost savings (e.g., reduced marketing) ($/year) _____ think and on the capacity of your business. Recommendations from highly influential people can rapidly accelerate your career and grow your business exponentially. One key to becoming influential is that your career or business must be capable of growing. It's one of the reasons many business experts recommend not restricting your business to being self-employed and charging by the hour. When you limit your business to the number of hours in your week, you have a limit to how rapidly you can expand as well as to the amount of money you make.

CHAPTER 3
Understanding Wildfire

"People love gossip. It's the biggest thing that keeps the entertainment industry going."
—Ellen DeGeneres

Never underestimate the power of word of mouth. Word of mouth is a driving force that can transform a one-on-one conversation to a one-to-many conversation with the speed of a wildfire.

What causes a wildfire word-of-mouth epidemic? What takes word of mouth from that one-on-one level—where your favorite customer will talk to his neighbor about you over the fence—to that epidemic level, where people you don't even know are talking about you on Facebook and Twitter? When word of mouth catches, books turn into bestsellers, songs turn into overnight sensations and "ordinary" folks turn into instant celebrities.

Wildfire makes a great analogy for how word-of-mouth turns epidemic. When I was young, one of my summer jobs was to run groceries to fire crews in northern Canada. This gave me the opportunity to see wildfires up close. Yes, they're a little scary; at the same time they're amazing forces of nature: great catalysts of change and growth.

The fire boss would always tell me, "Wildfire needs three ingredients—spark, fuel and wind. When you've got all three, we need a lot of groceries!" When you have all three, you're not dealing with a simple brush fire. The wildfire will be massive and beyond anything you can imagine.

In this new information age, ideas, trends, products or activities can start out as a single instance or occurrence and spread with epidemic rapidity into a wildfire.

Spark

spark (n): anything that serves to animate, kindle, or excite
Collins English Dictionary

Nelson Mandela is recognized throughout the world as providing the spark to light the life-changing fire of civil rights. A controversial figure for much of his life, Mandela was denounced as a revolutionary and terrorist by critics due to his anti-apartheid activities, eventually serving more than 25 years in prison. During his time in prison, Mandela was transformed into a leader who played the pivotal role in the dismantling of apartheid in South Africa.

The roots of Mandela's influence in Africa started early, with his law practice being one of the few refuges where black South Africans could turn to for help. Mandela first became a household name in Africa in 1952. At the height of apartheid, with significant threat of the Afrikaner government declaring the black African National Congress (ANC) an illegal organization, many of the leaders of the ANC, including

Pop Quiz

What catches wildfire easier?

a) Big spark

b) Little spark

c) Don't be silly, I never play with fire

Mandela, were under government ban from attending any meetings. Mandela convinced the leadership to draw up a plan allowing the ANC to operate from underground and was given the task of developing a plan.

The plan, which became known as the Mandela Plan, became both the basis for communication and leadership.

Ironically, in solving this problem for the ANC, Mandela became a household name among black South Africans. With communication controlled and little news coming through, a black South African in the 1950s might not know the names of the ANC leaders, but would definitely have heard of the Mandela Plan.

The roots of Mandela's influence began in the problems he solved: first tactical problems, and later the simple fact that he became the face of resistance to apartheid.

Big spark catches easy. Solve a big problem and the world will listen to your every word.

> *"Big spark catches easy. Solve a big problem and the world will listen to your every word."*

Influential people are visionaries; they are driven by their *why*, not their what. Influencers define themselves by their vision of making a big difference, not by the mundane of what they do or how they do it. Vision inspires; day-to-day activities do not.

Have you ever made the mistake of thinking that working on a big problem that's of great significance to others will be too hard? (Perhaps you practice on the little stuff that's not particularly important to you or anyone else.) Nothing could be further from the truth. The bigger the problem you solve for others, the bigger the service you provide, the more happiness or relief you bring, the easier it is to be the subject of wildfire word of mouth. That's why the expression, "The bigger the why, the easier the how" has become a popular quote among transformational leaders from Janet Bray Attwood's book *The Passion Test*[8]. *The Passion Test* is a great resource if you're struggling to figure out what to focus on.

Before you start planning your next online campaign or product roll-out, make things easier on yourself. Give yourself a really big spark. Regardless of whether you are creating a global movement or you are a business owner bringing a better product to your local community, if you are truly committed to being of service to others, your influence has the roots it needs to grow.

When I was a teenager growing up in North Bay, Ontario, we all knew the places that were legendary for fast food. Roman Villa makes the best hot banana pepper assorted sub on the planet, the pizza at Greco's is better than the best of Italy, and, of course, Paul Weber's burgers are touted with rapt looks of hunger. Every town has a list like this. The North Bay list is remarkable in only one thing: one of these restaurants is a two-hour drive from North Bay.

Paul Weber's is the subject of urban legend. Paul Weber built a walkway across the four-lane highway so that customers travelling south to Toronto could stop for a burger. The story behind the walkway is spoken of in hushed tones. Stories are told of near misses or actual deaths as rabid burger seekers risked or gave up their lives to cross four lanes of the worst traffic in Canada to enjoy a Paul Weber burger. Need I say more?

The legend has grown to epic proportions.

One fact remains: Paul Weber didn't want customers risking their lives for a burger. So much so that he was willing to pay substantial dollars for a parking lot across the highway and a skywalk across a four-lane freeway. Customers, inspired by this commitment, continue to create a wildfire epidemic around Weber's burgers – now an urban legend that has lasted some 30 years.

What's your fuel? To generate this kind of wildfire word of mouth, your fuel is the level to which you care about your customers, your suppliers and your business allies. How much are you willing to invest in them? The bigger your commitment, the greater your influence.

Exercise 4: Make Your Commitment Big and Public

1. Make a list of commitments to those you work with and for. Your commitments can be a policy for customer service, an ethic by which you work or something physical, like a walkway across the highway.

2. Make your word become your world! If you say it, be it! State your commitment loudly and publically—post it on your door, say it often, even create a physical representation of it. Giving your word publically will help you complete your goals, time and again.

3. Once you've gone to the mat for those you serve, celebrate your commitment in the media. Create a great story around your success and call a local reporter; write a press release and put it on your website so you can celebrate it for years to come.

Fuel

fuel (n): material such as coal, gas, or oil that is burned to produce heat or power; a thing that sustains or inflames passion, argument, or other intense emotion

Collins English Dictionary

"I have a dream."

Read those words, and you immediately know I'm quoting Dr. Martin Luther King Jr. from one of the most studied and quoted speeches in global history. Newspapers and television media around the world cover that important occasion.

Yet few people remember the first words of that speech. On a whim, I asked several friends, both American and Canadian, what they think the first words of that speech are. Half cannot even venture a guess. Two say "I have a dream." One guesses, "Four score years ago…." (which is close to the second statement of the speech "Five score years ago…."). One person inventively pulls up Google on her iPhone and accurately quotes, "I am happy to join with you today, in what will go down in history as the greatest demonstration for freedom in the history of our nation."

Search "Martin Luther King's I have a dream" on YouTube and watch that speech. You will notice something most people miss, including many of the historians and communications experts who have written long essays on that speech. For the first 11 minutes of that speech, Dr. King reads, purposefully and expertly, from his notes. His words are carefully designed and delivered to paint a clear picture, a clear call to action. Three times he makes a call to action saying "now is the time!" repeatedly calling for peaceful and respectful resistance.

Then at just past 11 minutes something truly magical happens.

Dr. King stops looking at his notes.

His emotional energy shifts and he becomes more grounded than we have ever seen him. Every cell of his being speaks his passion and he begins to speak entirely from the heart. There is no longer a glance at a script in front of him, just words spoken deeply and passionately. His passion is so great that housewives across the world talk about this being the moment they stopped working in the kitchen and walked over to the television set.

> *"So even though we still face the difficulties of today and tomorrow, I still have a dream. It is a dream deeply rooted in the American dream. I have a dream that one day this nation will rise up and live out the true meaning of its creed."*

King uses the phrase "I have a dream" seven more times before the end of the speech. Each sentence produces a vivid image of a reality that is right in front of us all for the taking. An image rooted in passion and belief and freedom.

In the course of a single speech, the world moves.

The fuel in your wildfire is how passionate you are in what you do.

> *"The fuel in your wildfire is how passionate you are in what you do."*

Passion sells.

Passion is infectious.

The greater passion level, the more engaging you are. People are drawn to passion.

The greater your passion, the more likely you'll be noticed in all forms of media.

Do not mistake passion for extroversion. Mahatma Gandhi and Nelson Mandela were both self-acknowledged introverts. Passion is the level of emotion you bring to something. It is not about how loud or how much you speak, but about how committed you are to a positive outcome.

Passion is grounded in your heart.

Authenticity

Being passionate about what you do is a big part of authenticity. Authenticity is something that is frequently talked about these days, though few people define it. Here's my definition: authenticity is your inner voice saying the same thing as your outer voice.

You can spot a phony a mile away. If your mind is saying, "Oh God, I need this sale," and your outer voice is saying, "This is a great product you should try," consider that everyone can spot you for the phony you are.

This is at the root of "The Law of Attraction": when your emotional

state is positive and passionate, people are drawn to you and want to help you. When you are inwardly focused on your own pain, boredom or fear, people are not drawn to you. Consider they may be repelled.

If you don't passionately love what you do, you have two choices:

1. Find a way to connect with why you love what you do, or

2. Change what you're doing.

Again, your *why* comes into play. When you're clear about why you want to influence change, the more you're driven by your compelling reason, and the easier you can influence others.

Passion can come in many forms. Though we often think of Martin Luther King Jr. when we speak of passion

Pop Quiz

Which of the following most accurately describes you:

a) You live to work, you so love what you do that you'll never retire

b) You work to live, you can't wait to retire some day

c) Shoot me now. I can't stand the thought of doing this work another day

Answer (a) is the answer that involves the greatest passion and authenticity.

that ignites, Nelson Mandela is another great example. His passion was quieter, though equally effective. Through tenacity and commitment to a cause, Mandela never gave up on his dream of an apartheid-free South Africa.

Mandela's passion arose from his willingness to steadfastly stand for human dignity and rights regardless of the consequences. And to persistently become the solution of whatever problem lay in front of him.

What gave this man the strength and wisdom to exclaim, "As I walked out the door toward the gate that would lead to my freedom, I knew if I didn't leave my bitterness and hatred behind, I'd still be in prison"?

Passion is magnetic in all its forms.

Wind

wind (n)—air in natural motion

Collins English Dictionary

Why do you trust your geeky cousin Alfred telling you which computer to buy, but if the salesman at Future Shop says the same thing, you want to shop around and do more research? The answer is obvious—people naturally mistrust you when you stand to gain in a situation.

More than likely, the salesman works on commission. And, whether or not he actually works on commission, you at least suspect that he does, so you remain skeptical. Alfred just really likes his particular brand of computer so there's no threat of false information.

Applying the principles of what creates influence to business is a challenge. Because, let's face it, if you're not in business to make money, you're not in business. There are plenty of charitable endeavors, but most people still need to make money. Having other influential people endorse your work creates the foundation of trust, even when people naturally mistrust because you stand to profit.

Wildfire word of mouth epidemics happen when many influential people band behind an idea and spread the word. Malcolm Gladwell's *The Tipping Point* refers to them as the Mavens and Connectors—those we trust and those who have many people who trust and listen to them.

***

It's just before 5 p.m. in New York, when Shawne ducks into a little café to get out of the noise and traffic. She's so happy, she's trying not to cry. I'm on the phone with her, my best friend, on the eve of her 48th birthday. And the word-of-mouth epidemic is starting.

It's been Shawne's dream for years to do a documentary on the topic of forgiveness. She's lived through some extreme challenges in forgiveness, being both an incest survivor and having close family friends killed by a drunk driver—the driver being a close friend of Shawne's family.

We're recalling three months earlier. Shawne's husband Terry and I are convincing her to jump off the metaphorical cliff and just start the documentary, even if there's no funding in place. We've all been working non-stop for three months to ask every influencer we know to participate in talking about the launch of a crowdfunding campaign for the movie.

What Shawne doesn't know is that Terry and I have been working behind the scenes to ask everyone to start early, the day before Shawne's birthday, the early launch of the campaign being her birthday present. Hundreds of influential people who Shawne has helped in numerous ways are champing at the bit. They all want to do this campaign for Shawne because they love her and believe in her vision. Shawne's generosity of spirit and all the energy she's given to others over the years is coming back to her exponentially.

I'm sitting on the phone with her while she sits in a café, watching the notices fly across her phone as donations come in.

"I'm so moved," she says, her voice filled with emotion.

"I've never been given a birthday present like this."

The wind in your wildfire is all those relationships you have with influential people. Who would you crawl through glass for? Equally important, who would crawl through glass for you? When you have worked to build up those relationships, influencers who love you will want you to win. They will become the wind in your wildfire.

In Part 2 of this book, we will be talking about the habits influencers have that lead to the depth and abundance of relationships that can create wildfire around your work.

PART 2
THE HABITS OF INFLUENTIAL PEOPLE

*"You can make more friends in two months by becoming
interested in other people than you can in two years by trying
to get other people interested in you."*

–Dale Carnegie, *How to Win Friends and Influence People*

CHAPTER 4
Here's the Overview
You Are Looking For

"If I had more time, I would have written a shorter letter."
—Blaise Pascal

I know many of you will browse through a book and look for a list of guidelines to follow. The "10 Habits of Influential People" are summarized below and further expanded upon in later chapters. Following the habits alone does not necessarily equal success, however, because you will also need a deeper understanding of the boundaries with each habit—the unspoken rules and common mistakes.

Unspoken rules follow each habit and some will be obvious while others will be easier to forget. Common mistakes include behaviors that would work for you in many situations, but not when dealing with the influential. These will help you know what to avoid.

Read over the habits, unspoken rules and common mistakes and consider reading them each day until every word is working to your advantage. The following is your list of etiquette to becoming influential; the wind that spreads the flames into a wildfire.

The 10 Habits of Highly Influential People

Habit # 1: Playing Big

Influential People:

- Are of high service to others (i.e., they solve a big problem for others).

- Focus on that problem to the exclusion of all else.

- Are confident. They know their fear is of no use to others.

Habit #2: Authenticity

Influential People:

- Do something they deeply care about.

- Only play with others they deeply respect.

Habit #3: One-to-Many

Influential People:

- Spend much of their time communicating in a one-to-many scenario (i.e., audience or following somewhere).

Habit #4: Influence is a Currency

Influential People:

- Use influence as a currency of relationship building, i.e., the currency of influencers is influence. Accumulate currency to spend on your relationships with influencers.

Habit #5: Building Powerful Relationships with Other Influencers

Influential People:

- Influential people assertively seek out and build relationships with other influential people who they respect and admire, regardless of the area in which they hold influence.

Habit #6: Understanding the Cycle of Reciprocity

Influential People:

- Build powerful relationships through powerful cycles of reciprocity.

Habit #7: Connecting the Connectors

Influential People:

- Consistently connect the connectors.

Habit #8: Become a Hub for Other Influencers

Influential People:

- Serve their community of influencers by becoming a hub for other influencers.

Habit #9: Engaging and Enrolling Others

Influential People:

- Are masters at engaging and enrolling others. They can sell an idea or vision and inspire you to take action toward it.

Habit #10: Influencers Take Action

Influential People:

- Routinely and repetitively take action toward their goals. When they do not know what actions to take, they take the action of seeking guidance.

Read This Next

You likely bought this book with a vision of something you wanted to create in your business or your life. Here is a way you can put this in action right now, as you read this book.

With the purchase of *Mass Influence*, you also received a complimentary tuition to *The 30 Day Influence Challenge*.

This fun, engaging online training course supports the learning you will do in this book by having you complete 30 daily, five-minute exercises. If you haven't already, please visit www.MassInfluenceTheBook.com to sign up.

Included with this program are downloadable versions of the exercises in this book and on-going daily influence builders. All are easy to do in two minutes or less.

CHAPTER 5
What's Your Problem?

"Possibility destroys the impossible."
—Charles Mulli

He is matter-of-factly sitting across the table, telling me about the environmental award he has won. At 5'7" and slight of stature, Charles Mulli is not an over-powering man, but his energy commands a room when he walks in. His wife Esther sits next to him with the quiet pride of a wife who is deeply inspired by and proud of her husband. Since 1989 Charles and Esther have been building orphanages in Kenya where they have adopted and schooled more than 7,000 children.

Maureen and Thomas Keller, who help run the Mully Children's Family Charity in Canada, have invited me for dinner so I can meet Charles and Esther.

"We have built a large greenhouse operation to grow food," Charles says. "The money from the operation provides many local jobs and the profit pays to run the school."

There is a twinkle in his eye as he tells me the story of the philanthropic business man from America who decided to provide the seed money for the greenhouse operation because he was so inspired by Charle's work.

"And now they have given me one of Africa's largest environmental awards," he laughs humbly, as if the idea were ridiculous that he should receive an award for doing what simply makes sense.

He pauses for moment and his face takes on a look of sadness. "Did you hear about the genocide we had in Kenya these past two years?" he asks.

I admit with embarrassment that the Kenyan genocide was not well covered in North American news, but I have spent a sleepless night reading about the killings in his book *Hope for the Hopeless*.

"A quarter million people were killed," he says with a look of resigned sadness. "But we went into the refugee camps and were able to rescue many of the children. We had no resources and only our belief that it must be done."

"However did you manage?" I ask, my own voice thick with emotion at the thought of what they must have faced.

"We believed in the possibility of what we were doing," he says and the twinkle comes back into his eyes. "Possibility destroys the impossible."

In that moment, my life changes.

***

How Big is Your Problem?

"The bigger the problem, the bigger the profit."

—common cliché used in business

Habit #1: Playing Big

Do you stand for solving a big problem in the world? Do you stand for solving a big problem for your organization—or are you taking the

THE WRIGHT BROTHERS DREAMING OF ONE DAY

stand that your organization is the solution to a big problem in the world?

To be taken seriously by influencers, it's important that you can articulate why you love what you do, why it solves a really big problem for others, and who your audience is. If you're missing any one of these elements, they will likely consider you an up-and-comer, a small player, and will likely put gatekeepers in the way of you approaching. Someone with high influence is judicious about who they help at a deep level. They have numerous people approaching them every month wanting help. Saying yes to all requests becomes a risk to their business.

Influential people tend to think, "Go big or go home." They are of high service to others. In other words, they solve a really big problem for others. Being of high service to others is highly authentic and of high value to other people.

> *Influential people play big. They are of high service to others. They solve a big problem for others, to the exclusion of all else.*

An influencer will focus on the problem they stand for solving to the exclusion of all else. You'll seldom find an influential person who has several businesses, unless they've completely delegated the running of those businesses or the businesses are closely linked.

Influential people are also highly confident. They know that their own fear is of no use to others. Influential people are not arrogant, they simply master the knowledge that fear can stop them and has little useful purpose in achieving

> ## Unspoken Rule #1
> *Influencers will not take you seriously if you play small when you deal with them. Have clarity, focus and confidence.*

their goals. Influencers tend to put their fear aside and deal in high self-confidence because they know that will help them be of far greater service to the world.

Exercises 5 and 6 will refine the work you did in Exercise 1.

If you are a student, this might simply look like taking on the courageous projects for your assignments. Or it may look like volunteering for leadership roles on different committees that serve the student body.

As an employee looking to further your career, you might volunteer to take on one of the biggest problems within your organization and focus on being of service to the other staff. Or you could look for a problem in your industry and volunteer to take it on in service to your customers, suppliers or the communities you serve.

Exercise 5: Finding Clarity

In your area of influence, answer the following:

1. What problem do you solve for others?

2. Do those you would help know they have this problem or is it a problem only you know they have?

3. If not, what would they say the problem they have is?

4. Who is your audience?

Defining the Problem You Solve for Others

Entrepreneurs have even more leeway. As an example, let's look at acupuncture, those who specialize in acupuncture know they can help people with arthritis, but people with arthritis don't necessarily know that the acupuncturist can help them. It would be far easier to be influential in the conversation of arthritis or pain relief or longevity, than to be influential in the conversation of acupuncture.

If you cannot define the problem you solve and who your target audience is, you're not likely to become influential. In business there's

Pop Quiz

Test your level of focus. Choose all that apply.

1. I run multiple businesses.

2. I tend to be great at starting things, and then move onto the next project quickly.

3. I like to have multiple projects within an organization.

4. I change roles frequently from boredom.

For any of these items you said yes to, you run the risk of decreasing your influence.

a common cliché: *if you're selling to everyone, you're selling to no one.* Your audience needs to be able to identify that what you're doing is for them. When audience and followers clearly recognize that you can help them, it will sway influencers to take you seriously as a peer.

I made this mistake early in my career with a reporter who had invited me to coffee.

She writes freelance articles for a major newspaper and several magazines.

"Tell me about your business," she says

"I'm a speaker and writer," I say. "I've started a charity to raise money for schools in Africa but my primary business is teaching

business courses. I have also written three children's books to raise money for my charity." I give her the full laundry list of everything I'm doing. I also mention that one of the organizations I'm involved in is a multi-level marketing training business that teaches empowerment courses.

She begins by asking me about the multi-level marketing company. I think it's part of the media interview. I tell her all about it.

It is, in fact, an interview of a different sort. She is assessing whether I am credible enough for a full-page article in a major newspaper.

She draws the conclusion that I am not. The article never happens.

An athlete who plays basketball, hockey and soccer is unlikely to make the major leagues in any sport. Those who have the ability to help you into the major leagues want to know you are focused on their sport.

> *An athlete who plays basketball, hockey and soccer is unlikely to make the major leagues in any sport. Those who have the ability to help you into the major leagues want to know you are focused on their sport.*

The Influence Game is no different. When you present yourself as scattered, people will see you as scattered.

Choosing how to introduce yourself is not about giving up all those sidelines that might pay the rent. But when you're in the influence conversation, they do not belong. Focus on the place you want to hold influence and bring nothing else to the conversation.

A common mistake in conversation is bringing in irrelevant points of focus. As an example, several times each month I have people contact me wanting to bring me into their multi-level marketing (MLM) business.

There are some strong MLM businesses out there. But if you want to hold mass influence, doing it in the context of your MLM is not a great idea. Why? MLMs are structured to be all about one-on-one conversations. They are based in referral marketing. Referral marketing is a valid game, but a different game than influential mass communication. Consider separating the two: making the MLM subservient to that area of your business you hold influence in.

For example, if you had an MLM that sold vitamins and you want it to become really influential around the topic of health, be in the conversation of health and health products, not the conversation of wanting people to be a representative for your MLM. Staying focused on your goal is critically important when you're approaching influencers. Otherwise, they're going to think you're playing a different game—making money with referrals as opposed to influencing many lives with mass influence. In this context, you're not going to be treated as a peer or someone who has influence.

Consider that in focusing on gaining influence around the more specific problem you solve, rather than signing people up to your MLM, you'll likely attract many people to your MLM as an incidental part of their relationship with you. People want to work with influential people.

Another way this mistake shows up is being all over the map in what you do. Do you have eight different business cards that pitch eight different products or services? When you decide who you want to be in any given conversation and focus on that one area you want to hold influence in, you will be far more effective.

Focusing on what you do to make money, if it's different from what you want to be as an influencer, is another example of this mistake. When in conversation, present yourself as focused on the area that's important to you. Spilling your guts and giving a full list of everything in your life is a time waster and presents you as a new kid in the game.

Take a moment and think about committing to the area in which you want to hold influence for the duration of this book. We're going to take the work you did in Exercises 1 and 5 to hone your focus. Remember, choosing your area of influence is a lot like trying on a coat in a department store. Sometimes you try the coat on and know you don't like the way the belt hangs or see that the coat's too short. The act of trying it on helps you see what fits. Consider this another exercise in tailoring the coat.

Now you might notice that what you just wrote may not be the same as the actual physical thing that you do, such as acupuncture or selling holistic medicines or engineering design. However, it's important to distinguish between the problem you solve and the actual product that you sell.

Exercise 6: Declaring Your Focus

1. Take an index card and write down on the card. "I am influential in [your topic]." *e.g., You might write "Environmental legislation" or "Helping kids who suffer from Leukemia" or "Bridge safety."*

2. "I am passionate, confident, and focused on helping [your audience]." *e.g., For your target audience you might say "the food growers industry" or "the elderly" or "women in business" or "people who suffer from arthritic pain."*

3. Then write "with [the problem you solve for them]." *e.g., You could write: "I am influential in longevity. I am passionate, confident, and focused on helping the elderly solve the problem of arthritic pain." or "I am influential in bridge building. I am passionate, confident and focused on helping city governments ensure cost-effective, safe bridge projects that last.*

***

In the movie *After Earth*, there is a powerful scene where Will Smith's character prepares his son to face the dangers they are about to encounter.

"Fear is not real," he says. *"It is a product of thoughts you create. Do not misunderstand me. Danger is very real. But fear is a choice."*

Fear stems from what you tell yourself about a situation. It is an inward-facing emotion of self-preservation. Much has been written about fear and fear mastery dating back to the earliest religious texts. It is reiterated here, so you can see the context of how it impacts you becoming influential. Fear is not focused on the present situation or on being helpful in the moment. Fear is an anticipation of a negative outcome in the future.

I often meet people who insist they have a positive inner dialogue. If that's you, I'd suggest you look harder. If you think your dominant inner dialogue is, "I can do it," check if you're really saying that in defiance of "I can't do it," which is the deeper inner dialogue you're attacking. You may have mastered the ability to dismiss your inner dialogue, but there's still power in recognizing what you're dismissing.

True influence is an outward-facing act. It is about service to others. It holds no place for fear.

Watch your favorite dog the next time you get a chance. Their attention is primarily focused outward on loving and bonding with others. They are masters at building relationships simply by loving and focusing on those they choose to be in relationship with. It really can be that simple and basic.

Humans, on the other hand, are hard wired with a lot of inner dialogue. It's one of the pitfalls of having language. To have influence, it helps to identify what your inner dialogue is and

IF DOGS HAD INNER DIALOGUE LIKE PEOPLE

59

Exercise 7: Build Confidence

1. Which of the following inner dialogues do you struggle with?
- I'm not worthy
- I'm not smart enough
- I don't have enough credentials for that
- No one would take me seriously
- I'm not strong enough
- I'm not lovable
- I'm too small to play with the big kids
- Other

2. Notice that all of these inner dialogues involve a fear of how others will judge you.

3. For the next day, every time you are upset by something, step back and consider:

a) What are you telling yourself?

b) What are you are making that situation mean?

c) Is the meaning you are putting on the situation empowering to you?

learn to accept and diminish this inner dialogue by becoming outward focused. Denying your inner dialogue, on the other hand, can turn that dialogue into a blind spot—something others can see easily, but that you are blind to.

Influence takes guts. It requires you to have a new take on a subject—something that is uniquely yours. There will be people who dismiss, despise, dispute, hate, or ridicule you and what you do.

I've been fortunate to have *New York Times* bestselling author Randy Gage among my mentors. No one makes it anywhere in the Influence Game without people who are more experienced investing in them.

Randy is a "tell it like it is, pull no punches" writer and speaker.

Randy does a lot of work in prosperity consciousness, teaching people to create wealth, and personal mindset. How do you develop the mindset of a multi-millionaire or a multi-billionaire? How do you change from lack consciousness to prosperity consciousness? When I spoke with him, Randy was clear that in order to do relevant work, he has to be in people's faces. He must call them on their stuff.

Randy talks about the programming people are getting from organized religion or mainstream conventional thinking—the government and the data sphere: TV, radio, movie, Internet, the blogs. Looking at what you've been taught as "programming" is often emotional, threatening and highly controversial to many people. He calls these mind viruses, most of them are negative and can cause people to self-sabotage.

I asked him for an interview for this book.

"What's the most important thing someone needs to know to step into the Influence Game?" I ask.

He responds,

"In terms of playing big, and being a person of influence, the most important thing is to have a point of view. That sounds really simple, but a lot of people don't have a point of view. Let's say they're a customer service person, a speaker or a consultant, and they read the ten top books on customer service and then they give book reports about what these ten experts have said.

Well, if somebody's in that space, they've already read those ten books. We don't need your book report or summary. We need to know, 'What is the insight you have that nobody else has?'

Certainly, whatever the field you're in, go and read the ten most influential books in that space. You should have read them and processed them, and then you need to bring your insight, the thing that you can bring to the table that nobody else can. When I go to hear a speaker, I want to hear a speaker who is the only person in the world who can give that speech. When I'm reading a book, I want a book where that author is the only person in the world who could have written that book. When I'm reading a blog, I'm looking for a blogger who's the only one in the world who has that viewpoint, that insight.

The thing you're going to have to really be willing to do, if you want to be a person of influence, is you have to be willing to piss people off. I promise you, if you're not pissing some people off, you're not doing relevant work. You're not doing anything amazing or epic. That's the nature of the beast.

There are a lot of want-to-be thought leaders, a lot of authors, speakers, coaches and consultants who pander to people. If you really want to have influence, you've got to be willing to tell people the stuff they think they don't want to hear.

The fascinating thing you will discover is that they actually desperately want to hear it, they just don't know it until they hear it. They've never had anybody challenge them, get in their face and say, 'No. The problem, the reason you're facing this problem, is because you created it. You have these beliefs or you're taking these actions or you have these habits —and that's what got you here. If you want a better result, you have to change that.'

You don't do it just to get in their face. I'm saying, where it's appropriate. Tell your truth as you know it. If you want to be a person of influence you've got to be willing to tell your truth as you know it.

Doing that kind of work, if I don't have someone every day un-follow me on Twitter, unfriend me on Facebook, block me on some site, unsubscribe to my blog, then I don't think I'm really being relevant. If you're doing work that's amazing, it's going to be work that threatens people. Because whether it's Marconi and the radio or Walt Disney's vision for Disney World and Disney Studios, writing a great opera, the great American novel, building the World Trade Center, founding your foundation to change the world—it's going to threaten some people if you're really doing something big, something that hasn't been done before, bigger, better, stronger, faster. The real innovation, that's change and people are afraid of change.

They may ridicule you sometimes, they tell you why it can't be done, they attack you sometimes. They try to talk you out of it. On my YouTube channel, I have a show titled 'Piss Someone Off.' It's really resonating with people because they understand, Wow, you know what? Yeah, if everybody around me is happy and everybody around me says I'm doing fine and everybody likes me, I guarantee you, I'm living a life of mediocrity.

> **I'm not responsible for the people who follow my work. I'm responsible for my work.**

I do it with love, I don't insult people to insult people, I don't shock people for the sake of shocking people. I tell my truth as I know it and I'm not responsible for the people who follow my work. I'm responsible for my work. And the work is the work. I don't defend the work. I don't explain the work. I'm happy to debate the ideas in the work, but I'm not going to defend it.

You have to be willing to do that.

What I can tell you is, my influence keeps increasing. My influence is greater today than it ever has been—even though I've been willing to alienate people who say they're going to unsubscribe, unfollow, would never hire me, would never recommend me.

When you're in your truth and you just do the work that matters, it's important to say you have the highest good in mind for your reader, for your seminar attendee, for your consulting client, for your coaching client—whoever your audience is—whether it's your citizens if you're a politician or your viewers if you're a television host. If you are coming from a good space, where you really are looking for their highest good, then people respect you and love you for the fact that you're willing to challenge them. When they come to your blog or they read your book or they listen to their speech, they know their mind is going to expand, they know their thoughts are going to be challenged and they're going to grow as a person.

And you know what? That means that they are influenced by you and they choose to be influenced by you. It's an extraordinary privilege and it's a privilege that comes with extraordinary responsibility."

This brings us to the final part of unspoken rule #2, "An influencer will not take you seriously if you are motivated by fear." Influential people are not arrogant or callous about people being nervous or in fear. Influencers know fear just like everyone else does. They have just learned to not be motivated by it.

> ## Unspoken Rule #2
> *An influencer will not take you seriously if you are motivated by fear.*

Influencers intuitively know that fear is selfish. Consider that your fear is all about you. In some ways fear can lead to a lot of very socially weird behaviors or personal dramas. Influencers often experience people approaching them and doing all kinds of nervous and odd things, like making huge asks of them before they've even been introduced. Fear convinces them that they will never get another shot at meeting them or asking them for a favor.

When you're in fear as you're talking to the influencer, consider that it changes the way you appear. It flags you as someone who's up-and-coming, not someone that they would take as a peer and highly influential.

There's nothing to hurry up and do. Relax. Build some relationships and what you need will come.

Recognizing Fear

Fear may be showing up in a number of different ways, such as: you're taking way too long to make a point or you're over-apologizing for something you're worried about. Maybe you're not talking enough because the fear has you paralyzed so that the influential person can't understand what you're saying.

Do some self-reflection.

- List the specific behaviors around fear that you want to stop and the behaviors around authenticity that you want to keep or start.

- Revisit this list daily, because you might notice different behaviors in different situations. Every day notice how you're doing because you want to become well-grounded into the most effective behaviors before you start connecting and building relationships with influencers.

- Start noticing your behaviors that have you show up as small. Consider that you are, in fact, a force to be reckoned with. You've got a lot to give to the world and you deserve to be influential. When you consistently learn to stand in that power and move forward confidently, influencers will start to take notice.

CHAPTER 6
Are You For Real?

"You can go kicking and screaming, or you can just go."
—Jennifer Hough

Habit #2: Authenticity

Confession time. I sometimes do business meetings in my garden while I randomly pull weeds. It's a grounding act that helps me stay tuned into the person I'm with and connected to who I am.

Pulling weeds is a symbolic act for me. It's a reflection of all those inauthentic parts of myself that don't serve me. Anything that pulls me out of the conversation or moment I'm focused on can create a conversation in my head that is different than the one I'm having out loud.

When I'm nervous, when I'm worrying about my schedule, when I'm stuck on being right, when I'm coming from a place of looking good, when I scold myself and stay in my own shame—all of those are weeds to pull.

They choke out the growth of who I really am in the world: someone committed to being deeply of service to others, someone who stands for others stepping into their own leadership.

Weed daily—moment by moment.

Anything that stops you from powerfully walking your path in life is inauthentic to who you are. They are

Weed daily—moment by moment.

random weeds to pull. Like gardening, it is an ongoing commitment, an ongoing noticing. It is not a task to check off your to-do list. The garden is not weeded once and then you are done. It is a moment-by-moment noticing of what has arisen that might need pulling to leave room for the flowers and fruits to flourish. I work on it daily.

Habit #2: – Influential people are authentic. Their inner voice agrees with what their outer voice is saying. They do something they deeply care about, and work with others they deeply respect.

The second habit that influential people consistently have is authenticity. People can spot a phony a mile away and they aren't going to like and trust you if they think you're a fake. You can become famous without authenticity, but it's very difficult to become influential.

The more you are aligned with what you love doing, the more you're

Exercise 8: What's Your Motivator?

Think for a moment about which of the following statements most accurately represents where you are at today:

a) I'm in my current line of work because it makes me a lot of money—if so, do exercises 9 and 10, or

b) My current line of work is my passion and I love helping people in this way—in which case you can skip exercises 9 and 10.

going to feel real to people, the more they're going to trust you. If your primary motivation for the line of work you've chosen is because it's high-paying or you think it's the best option available to you, then Exercises 9 and 10 in the next section will help you look at how to become more aligned with what you love.

If you're not sure of the answer, in other words, you're somewhere in the middle, it's worthwhile for you to do the upcoming exercises. Please don't interpret what I'm saying as "you can't make a lot of money doing what you love." Or that "you can't love money and pursue money because you love it." Though the love of money is not something I personally admire, there are people who have gained influence because they love money and are good at the pursuit of it. The focus here is on your primary motivator for why you do what you do. It's cliché, but it's important—do what you love and love what you do. Loving what you do is the foundation of authenticity.

Habit #2's unspoken rule centers on authenticity: "Influencers will not

> ## Unspoken Rule #3
> *Influencers will not take you seriously if you are inauthentic and only seek money or power. Know what you love and why you respect their work, as a peer, or they will lose respect for you.*

take you seriously if you are inauthentic and only chase money or power. Know what you love and why you respect their work as a peer or they will lose respect for you."

When influencers think you're only chasing money and power, they don't feel safe playing with you unless money and power is also what they love and chase. They will likely have their gatekeepers in the way of any relationship you're trying to build.

The number one mistake I see my students make inside the habit of authenticity is *not aligning yourself with your passion*. I'd also call this *practicing at business*. If you catch yourself making any of the following statements, you are likely making this mistake:

- "I'm just doing this work temporarily until I can figure out how to do what I really love…"
- "I've just started this smaller business to learn how to run a business, then I'll move into something more challenging I really love."
- "Once I make enough money, then I'll move into… That's what I really want to do."

Are you focusing on how you make money rather than focusing on the service that you want to bring to others? That's not to say being of high service won't make you a lot of money. Consider that if you're just practicing at business, if you're just doing some small "quick win" that no one really cares about, you're going to have a lot of trouble making money. Why? Because nobody really cares about what you're doing, including you.

I love the concept Jennifer Hough[10] and Sheryl Sandberg[11] both teach—to *lean in*. Far better to follow your passion and lean in the direction of those things you really love. You'll be much better at doing them, you'll solve a much bigger problem for others, and you'll typically make a lot more money because people will be far more willing to buy whatever you're selling.

Okay, I can hear what you might be saying right now, and you're right to say it. Yeah, everybody has to pay the rent. Isn't it okay to just pursue money at some point? The answer is absolutely yes, and no one who is authentic and of influence is going to hold it against you that you're pursuing money for the sake of money in some part of your life. The distinction is, if your only reason for pursuing influence is money, then you're into the realm beyond paying the rent. In other words, do what you have to do to meet your basic needs. But consider the risk to yourself if you trade away your influence for money. You will gain more influence when you align with what you really love, because that conversation is a lot more authentic to who you are. In the long run, you will likely make more money from having a higher level of influence.

If you don't know what your passion is, you can do some exercises to focus on finding it. I'm not going to tell you to quit your job, change your company or make any radical shifts in your life. I simply want you to find a way that you can align the area you want to grow influence in with the things you love doing. We're going to revisit the exercise we did in the last chapter. Skip this section if you're clear you're already doing what you love.

Your passion—that thing that will be easiest for you to hold influence in—probably lies in the convergence of what you love, what you're good at and where you feel most useful.

Leaning in

After I had my really bad year, the only thing I was truly clear on was that I deeply wanted to change my life.

I decide to "fake it until I make it". I look for the convergence of what I'm good at and the contribution I want to make in the world. I decide to take my hobby of writing children's stories and poems for my kids and write children's books to raise money for a

Exercise 9: Your Passion in Your Work

1. Write a few sentences on each of the following

a) What do you most love doing?

b) What you are really good at?

c) What are your natural gifts and talents that come effortlessly and seamlessly to you?

2. Now write a few sentences on the biggest frustration you've ever overcome. Some examples are:

- you've survived a divorce

- you've survived cancer

- you've dealt with bankruptcy

- you've failed in your business

- you've been laid off

- you've experienced not being taken seriously

Whatever that biggest pain or frustration you've ever overcome, that's something that's going to be near and dear to your heart. Write it down.

3. If you could do one thing to better the world, to really help other people or to really serve other people, what would that thing be? Feel free to dream big because when we're dealing with the influence world, the bigger you dream, the easier it is to create influence.

4. Look for opportunities that would be at the convergence of the above points. These are your coats to try on. Pick the one you think is the best fit. It's the one that excites you the most.

charity I'm helping create, which supports schools in Africa. I align my creative side with my desire to transform the planet.

I combine my work as a children's author with my knowledge of how to generate energy around a cause or idea, something I've done for much of my career. In less than eight months, all three books are on bestseller lists.

Then something quite interesting happens. Dozens of people start approaching me. "Three bestsellers in eight months! How did you do that, Teresa?"

I vividly recall the day, having a cup of tea with Shawne, venting that I'm not really enjoying being a children's author. I love writing the books, but going around to schools and doing kids' programs isn't really my thing. And I love teaching people how to create energy and influence around their work. But it makes me no money.

Shawne looks at me and says "Honey, if the universe is sending you a flood of something, maybe you should pay attention!"

Her statement turns on another light bulb in my head. I realize what I really love is helping leaders become more influential. I rebrand my business and change what I am doing.

I have never looked back. My life has been on fire ever since.

Consider the question: in what area do you want to hold influence? As you do Exercise 9, determine if there's a way to align your work with your passion. For example, maybe you're somebody who sells investments, but you love mountain climbing. You could, in fact, become influential in the conversation of mountain climbing and mountaineering and make great connections from people who would buy investments from you.

Once I realized my goal was to invest in and help grow thought leaders on the planet, creating the Evolutionary Business Council became an obvious next step. I only had to get past my own inner dialogue about not being worthy to lead an organization of emerging thought leaders.

Fast forward to the present day. My current goal is to have life-transforming principles reach 1.2 billion people on this planet by 2020 by supporting 1,200 emerging thought leaders to each reach and teach a million people. I chose this number for two reasons. First, my friend and EBC member Colin Sprake[12] challenged me to put a meaningful number to my, and therefore the EBC's, goal. I rolled up my sleeves and considered his challenge.

The second reason I chose it is because, according to the Law of Diffusion of Innovation[13], once an idea has been adopted by the innovators (the first 2.5%) and the early adopters (the next 13.5%) of society, it is simply a matter of time before that new way of thinking becomes the norm. In other words, the global tipping point for society realizing that we can control our own lives when we learn to question and control our own thoughts is roughly 1.2 billion for the expected global population in 2020.

I could never have conceived of this goal even a year prior. Big vision comes from leaning in to living what you love. The fact that I am passionate about what I do gives me the courage to stand in such an outrageous goal. It also helps that I surround myself with other big thinkers like Colin Sprake who challenge me to play big.

The more you can bring your work and your passion together, the easier finding your area of influence will be. Take a moment to think outside the box.

As you lean more in the direction of building influence in your area of passion, you'll find it's easier and easier to open up opportunities in those areas that will also help you make money. Consider that you might make a lot more money doing what you love than doing something that just pays the bills. When you are authentically doing what you're passionate about and good at, people and opportunities are naturally drawn to you. Your ability to sell goes up exponentially.

My colleague Kevin MacDonald[14], a business leadership trainer, is a

Exercise 10: Align with Your Heart

1. What is it that you love about what you're already doing? The more you can connect with doing it for reasons of passion and joy, rather than simply for the money, the easier it will be for you to build influence in the area of what you already do.

2. Consider changing what you're doing. You can do this in one of two ways:

a) The Radical Shift—If you feel you can take the risk, start up a new company or completely change professions. Sometimes a right-hand turn is liberating and exactly what's needed.

b) The Small Shift—Give yourself permission to do a little bit less of those things that you're doing just for the money to open up some space in your life. Then start doing certain things aligned with what you really love. For many people this approach gets you to your goal far more rapidly than the radical shift. The small shift might include focusing on doing the work you currently do with a group of people more aligned with your passion. For example, become influential at your hobby of working with immigrants as a means to bring in immigrant clients to your real estate business.

3. Choose one of the above options as you move forward with the exercises in this book.

great example of this. Kevin is a former golf club manager and loves to golf. He has combined his training business with opportunities to work with large golf clubs and spends much of the year speaking, training and coaching in the places he most wants to golf. His clients, large golf-related organizations, love working with him because he not only understands, but is deeply passionate about their world.

Think about holding influence in that area of your passion, so that you make it easy for yourself to eventually shift into that being your work or your business.

The second big mistake you can make around authenticity is not choosing who you want to play with based on fully respecting that person. Pandering to people who you don't really like simply because they have influence and power will not serve you and it will not serve them. Again, people spot a phony a mile away.

When Do You Walk Away from a Relationship?

Walking away from a relationship is a tough topic for me. I'm a recovering conflict avoider—I used to prefer walking away from a relationship over dealing with the conflict. And what happens in business reflects what happens in personal life.

If someone is treating you with disrespect, or you consistently disagree with what they advocate, there's a point when walking away becomes appropriate. Staying and pretending you don't care is inauthentic and an insult to you and them. Creating influence includes discernment of who you want to be in relationship with – whether it is your following, colleagues or personal relationships.

When an influencer ignores you, however, it may simply be a case that their level of influence is considerably higher than yours. The questions to ask yourself are

1. Have you invested enough time and energy to make the relationship work for them? and

2. Have you ensured there's something in the relationship for them? An example of this would be a reporter. If they reach millions, it may take years of helping them get good stories to sufficiently develop relationship.

If the answers are yes, then it might not be a fit.

When you can walk away in a mindset of kindness and respect, you are walking towards authenticity and personal power.

Choosing When to Walk Away

1. Have you been clear and simple about your requests?

2. Are you endorsing someone whose views or behaviors you don't agree with?

3. In the case where there is a significant difference regarding the level of influence you and they hold, have you invested in the relationship sufficiently to see if they would respond?

Bottom line, how does it feel? Trust your heart to know when it's time to walk away.

CHAPTER 7
Speaking to a Crowd

"It usually takes me more than three weeks to prepare a good impromptu speech."
—Mark Twain

Habit #3: One-To-Many

Do you deal with people one-on-one, or many at a time? One-to-many communication is one of the obvious habits of the influential. So obvious that it's typically overlooked in books about influence. It's the most common thing missing for people who could become influential but can't figure out why they're not.

Habit #3: Influencers spend much of their time communicating one-to-many.

Influencers spend most of their time communicating in a one-to-many scenario, meaning they've got an audience or a following.

The more influential the person, the more significant the following they have. The reverse is also true—the more significant the following, the more influential the person.

Because their time is valuable to them, they choose to communicate with many people at once. They typically have gatekeepers to make sure they use their time to its full advantage and reserve one-on-one time for highly important meetings that are of strategic importance.

The more influential the person, the more significant the following they have.

The average person can only maintain a social network of 150 close relationships[15]. Influencers sometimes have followings of thousands if not millions. They choose carefully who they allow into the inner 150.

How do you become one of those highly important people that an influencer would want to meet? Simply put, it's most effective to become one of them. Start developing an audience in some fashion so that you're playing the same game.

Leaders of large organizations are influential by default. The members of their organization are the equivalent of their following and are typically highly dedicated since they rely on that leader for their livelihood.

How influential a business leader will be is often dependent on the type of business or organization they run. Ironically, the most influential businesses require the least overhead relative to the amount of profit they create.

Creating an Influential Business

One of the most effective ways to move from one-on-one conversations into one-to-many conversations is by building an online presence. Online businesses are the simplest to run and have the lowest risk and overhead. There is no rent or mortgage to pay and little staff to hire relative to the amount of product and service that can be moved. They are the easiest businesses to turn into an automated structure. Building an

Business Type	Description	Bang for the Buck	Influence
Service provider	• *Trade your hours for cash* • *Their following becomes the clients they serve, which is limited by the number of hours in the week*	*Low*	*Low*
Business - Physical Location	• *Trade other people's hours for cash* • *Trade product for cash* • *Larger customer base than a service provider* • *Their following becomes the people who physically walk through the door (or live in surrounding area)* • *Expansion requires creating more physical locations with more overhead*	*Medium*	*Medium*
Business - Online	• *Trade virtual services for cash* • *Trade other people's products for cash* • *Their following becomes all those people they connect with online and is only limited by how good they are at playing the online game.*	*High*	*High*

online presence allows you to automate aspects of your business so that it can run without you. Most importantly they create the opportunity to have a large online audience that holds much influence. Automating your business gives you a luxury many business owners and leaders don't have—the time and ability to work on improving your business.

How do you move from self-employed into a powerful leadership role of communicating one-to-many? What might building an audience look like? Options for creating an influential role for you could include professional speaker, conference or committee chair, or newsletter editor. You might have a large social media following or host a teleseminar series or podcast. Maybe you're on traditional television and you're a reporter, talk show or radio host. There are even radio stations where you can buy your own show and sell your own advertising. As you'll see in later chapters, these audiences are not necessarily synonymous with your customers.

Working one-to-many does not guarantee you'll be influential, but it is near impossible to hold mass influence if you're strictly working one-on-one. This concept is so obvious many people overlook it. Having the one-to-many conversation is a critical element to holding mass influence because as long as you're dealing with people only one-on-one,

> **Unspoken Rule #4**
> *If you don't work in a one-to-many context, at least in one area, influencers view you to be playing a completely different game. Therefore, they generally don't want to play with you.*

a) you're not going to reach a lot of people, and

b) other influencers won't consider you to be playing the same game they are and therefore, working with you won't be a priority.

Exercise 11: Building Influential Connections

The spreadsheet for this exercise is included in the 30 Day Influence Challenge, tuition to which is complimentary with this book at www.MassInfluenceTheBook.com.

1. List ten influencers who are influential in the area in which you wish to be influential. This list can be a continuation of the list you started in Exercise 3 and could include professional speakers,

leaders of a professional group, event or a conference hosts, editors, magazine writers, bloggers, radio or TV personalities.

2. Number this list based on how accessible these people are to you. 1 being the most accessible, 10 being the least accessible. These ten names will serve as a starting point, because you will start contacting the "easier" influencers first. As you build relationships with them, they'll help connect you with the influencers who are more difficult to connect with.

3. Tracking your activity and conversations will help you remember important details. Set up this spreadsheet so that it can become a living document. I suggest setting it up on Excel or in your contacts database or in Google spreadsheets, allowing you to continue to add people to this sheet. Ultimately, this information will become part of your contact management, but for now, it's useful to see it as a spreadsheet.

4. As you're filling out the sheet, list the tools that those influencers use to reach their audience. This information will help you when you're connecting with them. You want to know what their strengths are so that you can meet them in the conversation that they're in. You might write things like, professional speaking, newsletter, Facebook, LinkedIn, etc.

5. Include a Notes section and fill in details of the last point of contact, so the next time you're speaking with them, you've got something to jog your memory. If you use a Customer Relations Management (CRM) system, I'd recommend you embed this information there.

Rank	Influencer	Who Knows them	Their Tools	Notes

Receiving Endorsements

Generally when top influencers in your field start endorsing you, your project or business starts growing exponentially. Remember the exercise you did at the beginning of the book (Exercise 3) where you estimated the value of an endorsement? My students often tell me when they do the work and do the work right, they've grossly underestimated the value of these relationships with influencers.

As you complete the upcoming exercises, remember to notice what starts happening with the number and quality of endorsements you start to receive. It won't happen right away, but stay the course and pay attention.

Playing Badminton on the Hockey Rink

Liz was venting about the arrogance of the women she wanted to connect with.

"She's so arrogant," Liz complained. "She thinks she's better than everyone else. She won't return my calls."

"Are you sure it's arrogance?" I ask. "Maybe she just doesn't see a benefit in the connection."

"I'm a good person," insists Liz. "If she doesn't see my value, she's just full of herself."

I can feel compassion towards Liz's venting. I've been there myself. Yet consider another possibility. If you're trying to build relationship with an influencer and you hold no influence yourself, you are trying to play badminton with a hockey player. It's easy to blame their lack of response on arrogance, but it is seldom true.

You may be taking their lack of response or communication as a personal rejection, when they're simply telling you *"You're not playing the same game as me, so it's weird that you insist that we would be good friends or people who should connect a lot. Why would a hockey player want to play with someone who clearly wants to play badminton?"*

Give up your belief that an influencer is being arrogant or judgmental if they don't want to connect with you. Generally people want to connect with other people who share their passion. Influencers are passionate about influence. If you're not in the Influence Game, they're not likely to put a high priority on connecting with you.

The Easiest Way to Work One-to-Many

The best way to connect with hockey players is to play hockey or become involved with hockey at some professional level. The best way to play with influencers then is to be in a one-to-many conversation. If you don't already have some tools for this, social media is the easiest way to start.

Most basic forms of social media—such as your Facebook personal profile, Twitter and LinkedIn—have you speaking to a broad audience all at the same time. You're connected to many and they are connected to many. It's like you're all equals at a big crowded networking event and all talking to each other.

It is a form of social influence. If you're well respected and well liked in that community, it does hold sway and influencers will pay attention to a certain extent. They may notice the number of Facebook friends you have. The limitation of social media is that they are not areas where you can be seen as a content expert. In other words, you're not seen

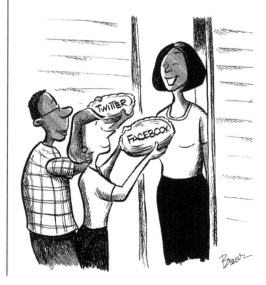

as the one expert speaking to many people at the same time. Influencers will not put as much weight on many-to-many tools.

Higher quality tools would be a podcast, a Facebook fan page, a personal blog or newsletter. These tools involve a single content expert who's known, liked and trusted by the audience and who is sending information out to a broad audience.

You may be sitting there saying, "I hate selling my stuff on social media."

Let me just assure you up front: your social media is not to sell you.

Social media, or other tools of influence, allows you to gift influence to other influential people. When you want to meet the new neighbor, you typically bring them a lasagna or apple pie. Your tools of influence become the nice gesture you use to meet and build relationship with other influential people.

We'll be diving into this concept more in later sections. Just know now that I won't be asking you to go out and promote yourself to other people.

Finding the Right Tool

Choose at least one tool in the many-to-many conversation (Facebook, Twitter etc.), and one in the one-to-many conversation (e.g., blog, podcast, newsletter). For the duration of this book, use the two tools you choose to complete these exercises. If you don't know where to start, I recommend Facebook because most of the planet is on Facebook. If you're predominantly trying to reach a business crowd, LinkedIn is the better tool for business.

Gear your choice of the tool to your personality. Do you prefer writing or speaking? Are you an introvert or an extrovert? Introverts or writers may want to lean toward a blog or newsletter, while speakers or extroverts might prefer a podcast a YouTube channel.

Ultimately, most influencers have many of these tools, and you can apply the principles to multiple tools, but for now, focus on improving your strength and agility in at least one area.

Hire Professionals

If you're just starting out and you don't know where to begin, a blog is one of the best tools out there for you to be seen as an influencer who's known, liked and trusted. They're fairly easy to set up on your own, but if you have the money, hire someone. You want to be

DOG TALK RADIO

focused on content creation and doing the things that create influence and make you money, not the tedious administrative tasks that other people are better at.

This isn't a social media book, although I will be giving you some tips and strategies. If you're really struggling on social media, I recommend you hire someone or take a course.

Grow Your Following

Focus on growing your following. Spend five minutes every day on exercises that are going to help you reach a broader audience. The credibility of having a following will help you be seen as an influencer in some capacity.

One tool I like is SocialBuzzClub.com, which was developed by Laura Rubinstein. The basic level for the SocialBuzzClub is free and it allows you to develop relationships with other social media influencers by sharing their content. Once you've built up enough points from sharing other people's content, you can submit Buzz of your own. You can put tweets and Facebook posts up and ask other people to share them. This is a great way to help you spread your expert content and grow your following. If you focus just on Twitter or Facebook shares, it's a great way to grow your number of friends or fans in your following. This is one tool you might want to spend three or four minutes on every day.

Most influencers love it if you repost a teaser to their articles with a link back to their blog. Reposting their stuff shows them you think highly of them and helps them rise in search engine ranks. Let them know when you do. Send them a quick note, or if you're posting on Facebook, tag them in the post[16].

As you start connecting with more and more influencers, it's going to be hard to keep track of who you've connected with and what you've been doing. I recommend keeping a record in the spreadsheet you started, so that you can recall your last conversation with each influencer – it will also give you a place to start the next conversation.

Exercise 12: Building your Social Media Influence

1. Choose one or two social media tools you want to focus on.

2. For the next week, spend five minutes a day using these social media tools to promote the content for the influencers on your list. Start with the most accessible influencers first. Look for their content and/or events and send it out to your following.

3. When you share their content:

   • Let them know you're sharing. If you're on Facebook, tag them in posts. If you're on Twitter, use their Twitter handle.

   • Repost their blog content. Of course you want to ask their permission first, but it's a great option for letting another influencer know that you are in the game, too, and are sending them positive energy.

CHAPTER 8
Show me the Money:
Influence as a Currency

"Let us not be satisfied with just giving money. Money is not enough, money can be got, but they need your hearts to love them. So, spread your love everywhere you go."
—Mother Teresa

Habit #4: Influence as a Currency

Every office has one: the super-nice employee who brings cookies to the office and remembers every birthday, then breaks down in frustration when they are passed over for the big opportunities.

There are two ways to look at this scenario:

1. The default belief is that all successful people are complete asses, mostly sociopaths and don't appreciate a nice, hard-working person. While this belief may be true in some cases, it's a limited view of the way relationships truly work.

2. Cookies and staff morale, while important, may not be what the leaders of an organization are looking for when deciding to invest in someone. Therefore, they are only somewhat effective in building relationships with the influential leaders within an organization.

We all have different ways of moving energy back and forth to create relationships with other people. For example, with your best friend, your currency might be that you listen to each other and help one another solve problems. Or you may have friends with whom you trade services, such as helping each other with projects around the house.

Influencers tend to use influence itself as the currency of building relationships. In other words, if the currency of influencers is influence, you want to accumulate this currency to spend on your relationships with them. Other means of building relationships aren't as meaningful. If you offer to buy them lunch or help them with home repair, it might be a nice gesture of friendship, but they're not going to value it as highly as if you give them access to other forms of influence.

The unspoken rule is: If you use anything other than influence as the currency of relationship building, the exchange rate will be quite high.

> **Unspoken Rule #5**
> *If you wish to play in other currencies, the exchange rate is extremely high.*

If you charge by the hour, an hour of your time may not be the same value as an hour of an influencer's time. That attempt will show that you don't quite understand the Influence Game.

Influencers powerfully build win-win relationships by gifting influence to each other. Examples of ways to gift influence include getting or helping an influential person get any of the following:

- Endorsements
- Powerful introductions to other influential people
- Audience members to their events
- Attention on social media
- Speaking engagements
- Interviews
- Connections to radio or TV personalities

Notice that you can already do some of the things on this list even if you have only a small following of your own.

It's not about score keeping or "you do this for me and I'll do that for you." It's an authentic give-and-take that happens naturally between influential people who respect each other—not unlike two best friends who naturally trust in each other's help. We'll talk about these cycles of reciprocity more in Chapter 10.

In later chapters we'll also explore the concept that traditional techniques for referral marketing and lead generation don't work well in the Influence Game. Any request that requires high time input, or high risk to an influencer's reputation, will likely be seen as evidence that you don't understand the game.

Asking influencers to sample your work can be a mistake: it can feel to them like a request, even if you intend it as an offer. Your book or CD might be great. But consider the following analogy—your children might be awesome, but you would never dream of saying to your new neighbor, "You're going to love my kids. You'll really enjoy babysitting them." You're

asking for a big time commitment from an extremely busy person, and unless your product is something that they would use or sample naturally in their daily routine, such as a beauty or food product, this kind of offer is not a great relationship-building technique because it has nothing to do with influence. Any time you offer something that's not influence-based, tickets to a sports game, a gift, or free services, they may be grateful, but this kind gesture will not have relationship-building potential. Consider doing something that helps them with what is really important to them, growing their influence and growing their reach.

CHAPTER 9
Your Relationship Capital

"When it comes to the fundamental issues that humanity faces, I think that solutions involve shifting consciousness towards cooperation."
—Jeremy Gilley

Habit #5: Building Powerful Relationships with Other Influencers

Watch the documentary *Peace One Day*.

It is about Jeremy Gilley's journey to create Peace Day—a day of global ceasefire on September 21 each year.

At first, Gilley does not believe he will succeed. His goal is simply to build a compelling story of how apathetic the world has become.

He starts speaking with U.N. officials to see if there is support for the notion. He then talks to Sir Kieran Prendergast, the then Under-Secretary-General for political affairs at the United Nations, to find out what would be required for the process.

The answer: support of many influential leaders. With the support of key people in the United Nations, Gilley moves on to talk with leaders in war-torn regions of Africa, travelling through Nairobi.

Gilley has a plan in place but then again he doesn't. Like most great endeavors, Gilley feels his way into the next situation, planning the next steps based on what happened at the last encounter.

As I watch the documentary I recall the words of an early mentor of mine. "You have to push the rope in the middle, Teresa."

"Seriously?" I'm in disbelief. "What fool would push on a rope?"

"Push the rope in the middle and run like hell," he repeats. "The ends of the rope will always follow."

Suddenly it makes sense.

An image forms in my mind of what he's saying. Find the people who agree with you. Forget the opponents. Just gather those who want to help and move forward powerfully. The rest will eventually be pulled along for the ride.

The highly influential know there is no gold in trying to convince the naysayers. Gather supporters and run like hell towards your goal. It starts with strong relationships.

> *The highly influential know there is no gold in trying to convince the naysayers. Gather supporters and run like hell towards your goal. It starts with strong relationships.*

Habit #5: Influential people assertively seek out and build relationships with other influential people who they respect and admire, regardless of the area of influence that they hold.

Relationship Capital

In business we often speak about physical capital and intellectual capital. An often-unseen asset is your relationships—I like to call this relationship capital. Influential relationships can mean millions in profit or positive results of any kind.

Influencers understand the notion of relationship capital to their core. There are two key aspects:

1. Influencers are clear with their boundaries; and

2. Influencers use tough conversations to build stronger, more intimate relationships with colleagues.

Yes, I actually said the word "intimate" in a business book. Try not to cringe and bear with me. I'm not referring to physical intimacy, but the emotional intimacy that comes from truly getting to know and learning to admire someone.

Think about what you assume when you receive feedback from someone influential. If they tell you your product is not ready to endorse or give you feedback about needing to learn certain skills and call them later, don't assume they're dismissing you. They may be investing in you.

A common mistake is thinking the feedback an influencer gives you stems from a place of arrogance or dismissiveness. They may simply be telling you the specific skills or tactics you are missing to become better at the game— or more importantly what they need to invest in a relationship with you. Consider paying close

Pop Quiz

Someone whose work relationship you value gives you feedback about how to better address his or her needs. You:

a) Add it to the pile of feedback you'll act on later if enough people complain,

b) Are annoyed and start thinking about where they're not meeting your expectations,

c) Jump for joy that someone is investing in a deeper relationship with you.

If you chose (c), you're on the right track.

attention. There's gold in that feedback.

A key aspect of building strong relationships is that influencers are clear with their boundaries. Because influencers routinely help each other, they take a great deal of risk in relationship building. Endorse the wrong person or product and their influence can plummet. The highly influential are therefore masters at the tough conversations.

When you watch Gilley's documentary, you'll notice that some of his best, most powerful moments come out of difficult conversations and awkward moments. A true leader's power comes from what they make of the breakdowns and difficult moments.

Intimacy is not a word that's often used in business. And it's appropriate to think about because there are people in business with whom you want a deep relationship. Tough conversations, where you share what's really happening and your true communication needs, are your opening to intimacy. Deep relationships lie on the other side of tough conversations. Influencers often have people who would crawl through broken glass for them, because of their willingness to have tough conversations.

Unspoken Rule #6

Building on the ideas in the last chapter, one of the major keys is that influencers who respect each other routinely offer opportunities for more influence. It's considered an integral part of the Influence Game in the same way that passing the ball is critical in football or basketball. It's a courtesy to their colleagues and they seldom have to shamelessly self-promote.

Influencers want to see that you know how to behave appropriately before they'll make connections for you. They want to know you will

> **Unspoken Rule #6**
> *Celebrate other influencers and freely spend your influence currency on those you respect.*

Exercise 13: Gifting Influence

From the inventory of influencers you started in Exercise 11, add a column and start making notes with each person of all the ways that you could gift influence to them:

a) For each person on your list, consider who you already know that's influential that the person on your list would want to know. They may hold influence in an area that's different from the one in which you're trying to grow influence. Don't worry about that. Influence is influence and influential people like to meet influential people, regardless of their field. Continue to add to your list of influential people.

b) Once you have your list in hand, ask the following questions:

- Can you recommend them for speaking opportunities or interviews?

- Do you have a Meet-up group or a stage on which they can speak?

- Do you have a podcast, video blog or Internet Radio show you could interview them on?

- Who do you know that has these tools that you could introduce them to?

- Could you celebrate their work on social media?

- Could you write about them as a guest blogger on someone else's site?

- Could you mention, repost or reference their content on your blog or in your newsletter?

- Could you write about them in your work?

- Anything else you can think of?

pass the ball before they invite you into the game. If you're not celebrating other influencers, people in the Influence Game are going to look at you as someone who's new and unskilled.

The following sections outline common tactics used in building relationships with influential people.

Introduce, Introduce, Introduce

What highly influential people understand is that introducing people, putting yourself in the role of connecting others, becomes massive relationship currency for you. Such currency is one of the most valuable assets for your business.

Consider that introducing people is making you money because you're building a huge asset. Move outside your comfort zone and practice connecting people. It will pay off in spades when you adopt this attitude.

Exercise 14: Create your quarterly action plan in an hour a week

Here is a plan of action that will assist you in spending your relationship currency wisely. Block the following times on your calendar so you will do them regularly.

Weekly—1 hour

- 5 minutes: Look at your tracking sheet of influencers and introduce some of them to each other.

- 5 minutes: Continue to track your list of influencers on your spreadsheet.

- 25 minutes (or 5 minutes a day): Work on growing your social media following.

- 5 minutes: Email at least one of the influencers on your list. Start with some of the more accessible ones, but challenge

---

yourself and email ones who you haven't met personally.

- 20 minutes: Set up a phone call with the person you emailed to introduce yourself and get to know them. Once others start connecting you, you will no longer need to reach out to people you don't know.

Quarterly—5 minutes

- 5 minutes: Visit LinkedIn and Facebook and invite friends to join, based on allowing LinkedIn or Facebook to read your contacts database. Increasing your connections will also facilitate you being able to connect people.

Email etiquette: Introduce yourself as a colleague and invite them to connect with you so that you can explore ways to collaborate. If they ask you to elaborate, simply say, "I'm a colleague in your field and I'm always interested in meeting new colleagues to see if there are ways we can help each other." If true, you can add "I may know people (event hosts, media) who would be good connections for you."

Most influencers will recognize that as a great opportunity to build more influence. Many will be happy to connect as long as you're respectful of their time. If it feels appropriate to take it beyond an email, a quick phone call, rather than a coffee or lunch date, is what you want to suggest at this point. These influencers now become people to add to your list and can be introduced to other influencers. If their level of influence is significantly greater than yours, however, I do not recommend any request that takes their time.

I recommend you ingrain these habits because they are some of the most important that you want to carry forward as you play the Influence Game.

Build Relationships Across Disciplines

An opportunity you may miss is to gain support from influencers you already know, simply because the influencers are in a different discipline. It's important to realize that you can gift influence into other topic areas, simply by the fact

> ## Unspoken Rule #7
> *Influence can be gifted to influencers in other topic areas.*

that you yourself are known, liked and trusted. Someone influential in health who recommends an amazing business expert, for instance, is still influential.

Attending Events—Influential Networking

Attending live networking functions is something everyone does. I want to focus on it because it's the place most people struggle in the

Pop Quiz

Pick which best describes you.

At a networking function, how many introductions are you likely to make?

a) None, they're big kids, they can introduce themselves.

b) You might introduce the few people you know, if you can remember their names.

c) You are a total wildfire—you'll introduce people you don't even know if they look lost.

Now let's do that same pop quiz again. You're at the same networking function, but now you're going to earn $1,000 for every introduction of two people you make at the event. How many introductions are you going to make?

Influence Game, especially introverts. If you're playing the Influence Game well, in the Pop Quiz to the right, you would have chosen (c), because attending events, both online and offline, is a great opportunity to meet influencers. If you chose (b), you're playing the referral marketing game, which is a different game with a different set of rules.

At a live event, the influencers include the host and the guest of honor. There may also be other influencers in the room and you can listen for the host or the guest of honor to identify them. Listen

Pop Quiz

You go to live events to:

a) Let loose and have a fun time,

b) Pitch yourself or your business to the people in the room,

c) Meet the influencers in the room and build relationships with them.

for the kinds of words that would convey influence: speaker, trainer, radio host, leader of a large organization, committee or conference chairperson. Any time they're speaking of someone in the room who speaks to a broader audience, they're pointing directly to the key influencers.

If you're attending a teleseminar or a group coaching call, the host and their key guests are the most influential people.

The host of an event is always one of the most influential people in the room. They've brought all the other influencers together. Your relationship with the host is foundational.

Make sure that you:

- **Respect your host's objectives for the event.** One of the biggest mistakes you can make is focusing on your own objectives to the detriment of the host's. Networking in the room with your only objective being to sell yourself or pitch your product and losing sight of the fact that your host has an independent objective will not get you invited back.

- **Be a gracious guest!** For example you often see people who own similar businesses going to a networking event where they know the host is trying to sell consulting or expert services. Have you ever seen a guest/expert in that same field start pitching people in the room? They're working to the detriment

> **Unspoken Rule #8**
>
> *Be a good guest. Assist the host and key guests in the room in creating a great event.*

of the host. That's a relationship killer for the person who's hosting that event. Other people in the room are not going to be impressed either. The host has gone to a great deal of effort and energy to put on that event and draw people there. Be considerate and present yourself as a supportive guest. Nobody's going to want to be in a relationship with the rude guest—not the host, not the key guests, not the other guests in the room.

- **Support the host by promoting the event before it happens.** They will greet you like an old friend when you walk in the room because you took so much stress out of their life. You can also bring people to the event, especially someone who might become a client of the host.

Endorsing and acknowledging the host and key guests is another way to be gracious. You can endorse them while speaking to people before the event in the lobby, or you can casually endorse them while asking questions, as long as you keep it simple and don't overdo it.

Here's a sample script for how to endorse a speaker while asking a question: *"I've been a huge fan of your work for so long. Thank you for coming and here's my question..."*

Offering value adds to the event can be another great way to support the host; just make sure you're honest and open about the win-win aspects of this type of offer. If you're offering your product in the room as a raffle or a free giveaway, the host will see that you are promoting your work. You want to have a really authentic conversation with the host beforehand to ensure this is okay. Springing it on the host last minute can cause embarrassment and disruption.

Here's a sample script for offering a give-away at someone's event: *"It would really help me out if you would raffle off or give away some of my products. Is that something that would support your objectives, too?"*

When you *become a connector* at the event, you offer real value. In the pop quiz about receiving $1,000 for each introduction you made between people at the function, how many would you make?

Option (c), "you are a total wildfire—you'll introduce people you don't even know if they look lost," is the one that's really going to support the host and support the other people in the room. If you help the host make everyone feel comfortable and make connections, it will increase your influence level in the room.

A key aspect of successfully making connections is to remember people's passions and interests. After you've met a few people you may think, "Hey, that woman I met 20 minutes ago would be a great connection for this guy I'm speaking to." You can actually walk across the room and introduce them to each other.

When you make sure people are introduced, it helps everyone have a great time and reduces the fear level in the room. For those guests who are nervous about not knowing anyone, you get to play the role of savior. They start to know, like and trust you.

A point that's often overlooked is that introducing people creates greater influence within the room as a whole. The more people in the room meet one other, the more successful the event will be because everyone will leave saying,

"Wow, what a great event! You won't believe how many amazing people I met."

When you generate that, your influence level increases significantly. You have been the life of the party at a highly successful event. People notice and remember you. They start paying attention to your work, they start trusting you when you endorse and recommend others. Their trust starts to become your influence currency.

Last, but certainly not least, it also increases the host's influence. Because you've helped the host create a great event that everybody's talking about, you've helped that host with their own influence level. They're going to remember you and know, like and trust you for that reason. Your relationship with an influential event host is initiated.

Help the host achieve his/her goals. Another key point for engaging people at events is to figure out what the host or key guests want to accomplish from the event and help them achieve it. They might be hosting the event to attract more clients or more members for an organization. Maybe they're hosting the event to create more influence or connections, or maybe the event is focused on increasing learning and they're building a learning community around them. Think about endorsing them openly

Making Introductions Between People You Have Just Met:

Introducing two people you have never met before might seem really uncomfortable. In fact, when you master how to make powerful introductions, it's like riding a bike. Let's say you've just met Raj and Kathleen walks up. You've never met either of them before, but they're both wearing nametags. Here's what you do:

1. Ask them if they've met. Give your best winning smile and you say, "Raj, have you met Kathleen?"

2. Acknowledge the humor of the situation. You're introducing two people you don't know. That's a bit whimsical. You can even try being a touch ridiculous because they both know that you only just met them, so you can say, "Oh, wow, you two really have to meet!" They'll know you're being funny, because they have not known you for more than two minutes. Or you can add with a smile, "I have no idea why. But I'm just sure it's true!"

3. They'll either take over at this point, knowing that you don't know them and they'll introduce themselves to each other, or

4. You can ask them questions about themselves to help them make the introduction. You can say, "Raj, tell us what you do?" Then you turn to Kathleen and ask her the same question, "Kathleen, what was it you said you did?" or

5. If you want, you can even be a little goofy to break the ice. You can say, "Oh, Kathleen, you're a brain surgeon, aren't you?" She'll laugh and tell you what she really does for a living. In fact, the brain surgery will become a joke that they can use throughout the event. It's going to release the tension, everybody is going to have a happier time and they're going to be grateful to you for creating the energy of that.

or walking their key prospects over to them so that they can meet.

When you're endorsing a host, you want to be authentic. Talking too long can be damaging. Say something genuine and appropriate but don't go on for more than 30 or 40 seconds. A decent endorsement is one or two sentences long. "Here are the key benefits, here are the results I've gotten and here's what it's meant in my life."

> *A decent endorsement is one or two sentences long. "Here are the key benefits, here are the results I've gotten and here's what it's meant in my life."*

Any time you're endorsing someone, the more results-oriented you can make the endorsement, the better. "Before I joined your group, I really didn't have any connections in this field. Now I have hundreds of connections and attract dozens of referrals every month, it's actually increased my business by $50,000 a year." The more you can make it specific and measurable, the more beneficial it is.

Endorse only when appropriate. If a speaker on stage is selling their products, don't interrupt them when they are in the middle of trying to achieve their goal. Others may think the endorsement was a plant in the room and it may damage the speaker. If you want to endorse them and the opportunity does arise to ask a question, ask and then add something like, "By the way, I've done your program and it's been amazing for me; thank you so much." Or wait and endorse them afterwards when you are near the people at the back of the room who are thinking about making a purchase. Timing is everything. Brevity is important.

If you really want to solidify the relationship with the host or the keynote speaker, record your endorsement on video and let them post it on their Facebook page or their website. They

> *Timing is everything. Brevity is important.*

will be grateful and remember you. It's a great way to solidify your relationship with the key influencers in the room.

One common mistake I see people make when they're at live events is forgetting that the host or the key influencers in the room are living, breathing human beings. The host has a great deal coming at them, so be compassionate. They're managing multiple details to put on this event, so don't overlook the fact that they might be a little stressed out. They might forget your name, or need a glass of water, or need someone to help them turn on the lights or close the door if it's too loud in the hallway. The more compassionate you are, the more you will be noticed and appreciated. Again these gestures aren't a substitute for gifting influence, but when you do both, the host will remember you.

Most importantly, hosts can get overwhelmed with feedback, especially at the event. Instead of giving them feedback, help them solve the problems For example, you could say something like, "Oh, I notice one of your volunteers didn't show up, do you want me to help with XYZ?" You will look like the gracious hero for having stepped in, and if that influencer knows what she's doing, she will make you look like a rock star for doing it.

CHAPTER 10
Understanding Cycles of Reciprocity

"Giving is not a strategy. It's a way of life."
—Bob Burg

Habit #6: Creating Cycles of Reciprocity

Something Robert Cialdini talks about a great deal in his work is the rule of reciprocity. When someone gives to us, we feel more inclined to give something back or to buy from them. Sales reps have been using aspects of this habit for centuries, giving free samples, or treating customers to food and so on.

When it comes to the Influence Game, this concept goes even deeper. Highly influential people create powerful cycles of reciprocity with other influencers they admire and want to be in a relationship with.

What Is A Cycle of Reciprocity?

Let's start with talking about what a cycle of reciprocity is. This term was coined and defined by Shawne Duperon. It's the natural cycle of give and take that happens in an extremely solid relationship; it's like breathing in and out, there's a natural back and forth to it, a lot like volleying a ball back and forth. In other words, when we converse back and forth, there's a natural *you speak/I speak, you give/I give, you listen/I listen* that happens in a really powerful relationship. It's not necessarily based on timing, but there's generally a flow of energy back and forth.

The basic rule of reciprocity (Cialdini) is that the feeling of obligation to reciprocate will outweigh a person's personal opinion of the giver. In other words, if they've done something for you, you will feel obligated to do something for them whether or not you like them. Cialdini notes that the principle of reciprocity, without relationship, can be used to manipulate and can kill relationships. A powerful cycle of reciprocity (Duperon), where true relationship building is occurring, goes far beyond feelings of obligation. Mutual respect and admiration build within the cycle. Obligation takes a back seat to generosity. Powerful relationships, then,

> *Powerful relationships are based on having a powerful cycle of reciprocity.*

are based on having a really powerful cycle of reciprocity. In short, influential people build powerful relationships through understanding

THE FIRST CYCLE OF RECIPROCITY

and creating powerful cycles of reciprocity with other influencers.

Deep relationships based on powerful cycles of reciprocity with other influencers are critical in the Influence Game. I recommend being intentional, focused and going deep in understanding this skill. To gain mastery, watch what works and what doesn't.

If this is an area you struggle with and a skill you would like to acquire, Shawne Duperon is the master at teaching this. I suggest you check out some of her free resources at ShawneTV.com and, if you have the opportunity, attend one of her "Networking is for Neanderthals" workshops.

Notice that I'm gifting influence to another expert. That's part of the cycle of reciprocity I hold with Shawne. Shawne has, in fact, become my best friend and is someone whose work I deeply admire. The cycle of reciprocity between us is so strong, I would literally crawl across broken glass for her. If I often quote her work in this book, it's because I feel so strongly and so deeply in the integrity and value of her work, and I trust you'll forgive me.

Unspoken Rules and Mistakes

Do the exercise on the next page before you read this section. Are you noticing a disconnect? Most people would circle all the responses in either parts of this exercise. Here's the challenge: you may find it strange when people you barely know ask you for significant favors. You haven't had the time to know, like and trust them and at the same time they're asking for something that requires trust. As a successful business owner or leader, you're also programed to "get out there and ask!" Many business trainers might actually tell you to just be courageous and do those things I've listed in Part 1.

Big disconnect.

Pop Quiz

Are you strange around important people?

Which of the following do you find surprising and uncomfortable:

a) Your new neighbor asks to borrow your lawnmower within minutes of meeting;

b) Someone you just met at a networking function asks you to recommend them on social media;

c) Someone you just met asks you to connect him or her to your most important connection so they can ask them for something.

Now, which of the following do you believe:

a) Ask and ye shall receive;

b) If you don't ask, you don't get;

c) The early bird gets the worm.

The Premature Ask

Imagine what this might look like in your everyday life. You've just moved into your new house. The neighbor stops by and comments on how nice your lawn mower looks. He gives you his best winning grin and tells you how much he's looking forward to borrowing it and your other yard tools. You look for an exit, but there isn't one. You're at your house. You tell him you're busy and make a mental note to figure out how to block him from coming over in future.

It's easy to understand when we're talking about a lawn mower. Yet I've often seen people at events run up to the speaker and inundate them with, "Oh, my God, it's such a miracle that I met you… I'm so glad I met you… You're the answer to all my prayers! I'm looking for an endorsement… I'm writing a book… I really want to meet this colleague of yours… and you're the answer to what I need. I'm hoping that I can buy you a coffee and you can give me an hour of free coaching for the price of a Starbucks so you can solve all my problems."

Now, I'm paraphrasing and exaggerating for the purpose of making a point, but this is tragically common. I, too, have made this mistake more than once.

Before you move forward, just forgive yourself already. You were just following your natural programming and all the training you've had to get out there and ask. Nothing you've done is wrong. There is simply a more effective way.

Human nature would have us excited and nervous when we meet someone who's important. It takes self-awareness and practice to re-wire this tendency.

A lot of people act like they're on *Beat the Clock* and they have to rush up there and make their ask because the influencer's only there for one day, and "if I don't blurt out my ask quick enough, I'm going to miss my opportunity."

Consider a different way of thinking. Yes, I want you to run up and meet the speaker. But do it to create a relationship with them. Offer them something that builds relationship. When you're playing *Beat the Clock*, make your dominant thought "I can take this opportunity to build this relationship." Suddenly you're no longer under a time crunch because now you're in conversation with this person. You've done something nice for them.

You always want to start with an offer of support. Never start with a request. This allows you to nurture and grow trust in the relationship. Don't ask until the influencer makes an offer. You know they're ready when they offer something back.

You might need to offer many times before the reciprocal offer comes back.

> **Unspoken Rule #9**
> *Don't ask until the influencer makes an offer.*

The more important a connection is to you, the more likely you are to feel the desperate need to blurt out your ask for support without taking any time to let them know, like or trust you. When starting work on the documentary movie *Your Second Fifty*, Frank Moffatt received literally thousands of requests from people he'd just met to be in the movie. At the same time, he had a handful of influential people call and offer support in promoting the movie or connections to possible funding sources. Which of these do you think gained his attention more rapidly?

It's really that simple. *Stop selling yourself.* When you invest in relationships with influencers you authentically admire, you invest in your own credibility.

Before you move to the next section, I suggest ordering Bob Burg and John David Mann's book *The Go-Giver*[18.] It's one of the best books you'll ever read. Once you have, you'll never make a premature ask again.

> *Stop selling yourself. When you invest in relationships with influencers you authentically admire, you invest in your own credibility.*

When to Move On

What if you've been working to build a relationship with an influencer and they don't ever offer something back? This brings us to the next unspoken rule.

If the influencers don't offer back, then one of two things are at play. The first possibility is that the relationship may not be a fit. You're dealing in different spheres, or your styles or goals are too different. Simply move on.

Unspoken Rule #10

If the influential person you are building a relationship with does not offer back, one of two things is happening

a) they are not a fit and you can move on; or

b) your levels of influence are so different, you need more investment first.

The second possibility is that the relationship may not be a fit at this time. The influencer may be too busy or the timing may not be right. Maybe their mother just died. Possibly your levels of influence are too far apart. Someone who's significantly higher in influence than you may want more evidence that you can play the game effectively before they invest in a relationship with you.

It's a human condition to have trouble hearing "no", especially from an influencer. Whatever their reason, there's power in accepting the word no.

One of the worst mistakes you can make is to create a big story around the "no" in making it mean something. Maybe you think it means they're arrogant. Or it means you've lost your big shot. It may mean very little. Consider that accepting the "no" graciously solidifies the possibility for later.

Be gracious and understand the power in taking "no" for an answer. Gracefully accepting a "no" is a position of self-confidence and power. There are many other influencers out there who are a fit for you; you just have to look. Accepting a "no" increases the likelihood of that influencer helping you connect with the influencers who are a fit.

Understanding the Value of Time

Disrespecting an influencer's time stops the cycle of reciprocity. Whatever you ask, make it easy and time-efficient. Every influential person has people asking them for testimonials. If you want a testimonial from an influencer, pre-write an example and send it to them.

> ### Unspoken Rule #11
> *Time is our most valuable asset.*

Now, it may sound arrogant to you, but it's far better to risk sounding arrogant than to ask too much of the influencer's time. The influencer is perfectly free to tweak or change the testimonial that you've written, but if they've got something to react and respond to, it's going to make it a lot easier for them. It turns what would be a 10-minute task into a one-minute task, which they're far more likely to be okay with. You might even be pleasantly surprised. They may send back the testimonial exactly as you've written and say, "Great," or they might write something even better. Go ahead and pre-write the testimonial.

The big question here is: when do you get to the point where it's okay for you to make asks of them, especially really time-consuming asks? I recommend you create a strong relationship with an influencer before

you make a request like this.

For example, asking an influencer for advice on coaching is a big time drain. I recommend you create a strong relationship with an influencer before you make a request like this. If you're asking for advice, make it something they can offer in a quick email or two-minute phone conversation.

Asking them to come speak for free is a time-consuming ask, especially if there's nothing in it for the influencer. If you're not creating a scenario where they can make money—such as being able to sell their courses or their products in the room—this is a huge time drain. It's their time to commute to and from the event, plus the time at the event and there's usually a certain amount of preparation before and follow-up afterwards, because people are contacting and emailing them.

To make this kind of ask, you want to be in a deep relationship with the influencer. The exception to this might be when you are supporting a really big cause they care about—asking someone to speak for a charity that's very near and dear to their heart, for example. Otherwise, this kind of ask is likely to put off the influencer.

Putting Someone's Influence at Risk...

There are a few ways you can put an influential person's influence at risk.

1. Asking for endorsement of low quality work

If you're asking for an endorsement on a book or an event, make sure that it's been well reviewed, you've had quality feedback, and quality work has been produced. You are asking an influencer to put their name to that, and it's a risky proposition. Your failure becomes

> **Unspoken Rule #12**
> *Never put someone's influence at risk in any way.*

their failure. Be careful and don't overreach, because not only will you significantly damage your relationship with that influencer, but also your relationship with any other influencer who may be witnessing.

2. Asking for something before you're ready

I'm all for standing in your power and confidence, but asking an influencer to recommend you to speak on a stage to 500 people when you've never even spoken on a stage to 20 people is not a good idea. This is a totally new experience for you for which you're not trained. You could easily make the person who recommended you look bad. Prepare yourself and earn the right to be on that stage of 500 before asking.

A little bit of stretch is encouraged, as long as you're clear with the influencer that it is a little bit of stretch. Make your asks in a reasonable progression.

3. Asking them to help promote or to speak at a poorly-run event

If an influencer offers to help promote or speak at your event, they are staking their reputation on your success. When the host starts half an hour late, is sloppy on stage, the sound system doesn't work, they're lackadaisical about people's time and the event ends an hour late, this makes the influencer look bad. Being disrespectful of people's time is the number one issue that annoys audiences. Like many speakers, I learned this one the hard way in the early part of my speaking career.

If you're asking influencers to help promote you, the responsibility is on you to make sure you're putting on a high-quality event. Your failure reflects negatively on them and you.

CHAPTER 11
Connecting the Connectors

"A tribe is a group of people connected to one another, connected to a leader, and connected to an idea. For millions of years, human beings have been part of one tribe or another. A group needs only two things to be a tribe: a shared interest and a way to communicate."

—Seth Godin, *Tribes: We Need You to Lead Us*

Habit #7: Connecting the Connectors

Connecting the connectors will transition you from neophyte to expert in playing the Influence Game.

In Chapter 1, you looked at how to play big in a problem others want you to solve. In other words, what's that reason people fall in love with you? What's the problem you solve that's a major challenge in their life?

Then you considered the realm of working in the one-to-many, moving out of working one-on-one, like a consultant or a contractor, and reaching a broader audience.

Next, you focused on influence being the currency of influencers. To really step into the Influence Game, you learned how to effectively trade influence back and forth.

Then you worked on skills for networking with influencers.

Finally you looked at the most powerful skill you could have, how to effortlessly and effectively create cycles of reciprocity with influential colleagues.

If you've been working through the exercises and solidifying all the skills we've covered to this point, what's in this chapter should not seem like a big stretch. It's been referenced several times and you've likely already started doing it as you've progressed through the exercises.

Influential people consistently connect other connectors. In other words, they connect people who are far more influential than they are.

When you become a connector of connectors, it starts to ramp up your game. This is where you start building that golden Rolodex of amazing people ready to blast out for you or support your work, and it's the quickest way to building a large mailing list. As long as you're in a strong relationship with other connectors, and have many people sharing your free programs or your newsletter, you'll build that large following in record time.

Writing Introductions

Introducing the influential to one other involves etiquette. A common mistake I often see my students make is to only introduce one party, making the assumption that the more famous of the two is obviously known. This creates two issues. First, it puts the two people you're introducing on an uneven playing field. It's like announcing that one of them is more important to you. Second, your assumption may not be

Exercise 15: Add to Your Weekly Action Plan

Weekly

- 5 minutes: Make one email introduction of two influential people a week. (For you over-achievers, do one a day).

true and may create discomfort. It's gracious to introduce both parties. Have fun and try to impress each of them with the other's credentials. That sets the stage for strong collaboration and mutual respect between them.

If you're asking an influencer to introduce you to another influencer, provide them with a pre-written introduction for yourself.

Since someone else will be delivering the introduction on your behalf, it's acceptable to "big yourself up" in the introduction. Send a well-crafted introduction to make it easy for them to introduce you. They don't have to think about what they're going to say, only how they're going to introduce the two of you. For example, here's what I might send to someone from whom I've requested an introduction:

"Please meet Teresa de Grosbois, four-time bestselling author and international speaker. Teresa teaches people how to create word-of-mouth epidemics. She's also founded an international

invitation-only council of thought leaders who collaboratively work to help each other grow their influence in order to make the world a better place. You two have much in common, so I wanted to connect you to look at possible collaborative opportunities."

CHAPTER 12
The Hub

"If not me, then who? If not now, when?"
—Hillel the Elder, Ancient Babylonian leader

Habit #8: Become a Hub for Other Influencers

A more advanced form of connecting the connectors involves bringing together and serving the greater community of influencers in your field. High influencers serve their community of influence by becoming a hub for other influencers. Bringing the community together will help you build that golden Rolodex of influencers and the massive following that comes from others seeing you as someone who is of high service to the influential. You become someone who others pursue because they see you as a leader in their industry - the quintessential mover and shaker.

Large campaigns, teleseminar series and multi-speaker events, all become easily possible—either as a host or a guest—when you become the hub. As the hub, attention and focus start to move toward you.

You can do this on a small scale or a big scale; it's up to you. Remember, you are just trying on coats. This is the one of the best coats you can choose. Even if the concepts and exercises in this section feel like they might not be a fit for you, try them out at least on paper and in conversation. You can make the decision not to follow through later, but do the initial parts of these exercises because they will help you understand where big influence comes from and how to move into the Influence Game on a larger scale.

Even if the concepts and exercises in this section feel like they might not be a fit for you, try them out at least on paper and in conversation. You can make the decision not to follow through later, but do the initial parts of these exercises because they will help you understand where big influence comes from.

Become Influential By Gathering Influencers

The person who brings other influencers together gains a level of credibility equal to or even above those they gather. It's easy to confuse expertise with influence, but they are distinct. In other words, your expertise might not be equal with some of those you gather, but your level of influence will be.

> ### Unspoken Rule #13
> *The person who brings other influencers together gains a level of influence equal to or above those they gather.*

Oprah Winfrey was on the air for 25 years with the most popular talk show in history and is arguably the most influential woman in the world. Oprah became influential by gathering influencers together in various conversations—health, spirituality and personal empowerment. She herself started to be seen as influential in the conversations of health, spirituality and empowerment, even though many of her guests were more educated in those fields. Because she's a hub, because her reach is much bigger, she's far more influential, even though her expertise may not be as great.

How To Become A Hub

When working to become a hub of influencers, be careful not to work with experts who are so insecure about their own credentials that they will damage your credibility. Work with influencers who will help you, not stand on your shoulders and push you down.

Never let someone you're helping hurt your credibility by talking down to you or acting like you are not his or her equal. Everyone has different strengths. Having greater expertise in one area doesn't mean you don't have greater influence in that conversation. You're doing them a favor by helping them and giving them influence. They should not do you a disservice by talking down to you or dismissing you in any way, especially if they're on your stage, engaging in one of your teleseminar series or participating in any public event.

Consider who you want to play with and become discerning. People who don't understand the concept of creating powerful cycles of reciprocity, of respecting and preserving each other's credibility and reputation are going to harm you in the long run. You also don't want to be recommending them to other influential people since they'll harm your colleagues' credibility as well.

Be careful not to give away your personal power because you think you're not smart enough, big enough or important enough to connect other influencers. People just starting out in a specific industry or conversation can become highly influential very rapidly because they have the courage to connect the big influencers.

You don't have to be the smartest person in your industry to be of service and create influence. It simply takes guts and an understanding of the rules. You become a leader within your industry by coming from a place of service and generosity. Be of high service to the influencers around you and you'll find that influence flows to you rapidly.

Consider that everyone else may be suffering from the same self-doubts as you.

I spoke about starting the Evolutionary Business Council for years before I had the guts to take the leap. Who could ever be big enough, smart enough, influential enough to create a community of thought-leaders and emerging thought leaders? Finally some of my closest colleagues did an intervention on me. They simply asked, "So when are you going to do that, Teresa?"

I immediately knew that the answer was "now."

Not surprisingly, those same colleagues became the first Board of Directors for the organization.

There are probably dozens of people wishing there was a great connection of the experts and influencers in that field, but none of them feels quite big enough to be the one who connects them all together. Try it and watch what happens. You'll be amazed how rapidly your own influence grows.

Designing a Hub of Connectors

What would it look like if you were to become a hub of connectors in your industry or area of expertise? We'll work through your design in Exercise 16.

Answer the following:

1. WHAT: First of all, decide if it is going to be a formal or an informal community. Choose what you're most comfortable with; you can always change your mind later.

Secondly, what type of community do you want to create? Your community can range from a mastermind to a large network of other influencers.

Generally a **mastermind** is six people who routinely meet in person or by phone. The concept was first written about by Napoleon Hill.

Each person is given a specified period to talk about their needs and what they're trying to generate. The other five people on the mastermind do everything they can to assist that person in those needs. The most common structure is six people, who meet on the phone once a month for an hour and each person is the focus of conversation for eight to ten minutes.

Masterminds are a powerful business tool. If you're the creator of the mastermind, you inadvertently gain a level of leadership and respect and become an integral component.

A second form of influential hub would be to create a **learning community**, where you bring many people from your area of expertise together to collaborate and learn from one another, tackling questions such as what works in your niche market, what doesn't and how to market or grow your businesses.

A learning community can be run live, such as conferences, meet-up groups and training events, or online, such as hosting webinars and teleseminars that you would share with each other, creating an environment where you could all learn together.

A **network** is another form of hub. Networks work well for people who want to do referral marketing; they're looking for one-on-one clients or people with whom to consult. Networking groups are where people go to make connections in business, but it's not necessarily connection with other influencers, so it's a specific type of community.

A council is the final option. It's a many-person group with a specific objective. Generally a council is about solving a specific problem for people or intensely looking at a specific topic area.

2. WHY: The next factor you have to determine is why you exist:

- What's the problem you solve for your industry, your area of expertise?

- What's the problem you solve for the other influencers?

For example, if you were focused on cancer and cancer research, the problem that you solve for the public at large might be better information or better information dissemination on cancer prevention and cure. You might also focus on after-care or family support.

3. THE OUTCOME: What is the outcome that you create as a group? It might be a world without cancer or a world where cancer sufferers have better access to the resources and support they need. It might be a different approach to operating in business or sustainability in a certain industry. Choose the outcome that your group is creating so that everyone has a clear picture what they're signing onto when they join.

4. LOGISTICS: Finally, decide the logistics:

- How often you meet and for how long?

- Who would be involved?

- Who would you invite to join your community?

- Who would facilitate the meetings or run the group?

Exercise 16: Design a Conceptual Hub of Influencers for What You Do

What would it look like if you were to become a hub of connectors in your industry or area of expertise?

Answer the what:

- Formal
- Learning Community
- Mastermind

- Informal
- Network
- Council

Why:

What is the problem that you stand for the solution of?

_____

Where:

- Live Location
- Online Location

When:

- One-time event
- Weekly
- Monthly
- Annual

Who:

- Leadership
- Marketing Partner
- Speakers or experts

- Membership
- Other

- Where are you going to meet? (Online, teleconference calls, webinars, offline in a physical location? Are there going to be meet-ups in your community or are you going to have a big conference somewhere that everybody meets at?)

Be creative and think of as many ideas as you can. If you can't specifically choose between two options, then pick both for now. Move forward in the conversation that you're debating between A or B and flush out both. The process of beginning both will show you which one feels like a better fit for you.

CHAPTER 13
Rock 'n' Enrollment

"The most important innovators often don't need any technologies - just imagination and acute sensitivity to people's needs."
—Geoff Mulgan

Habit #9: Influencers Are Masters at Engaging and Enrolling Others

Now you have an idea of what community you might want to create, it's time to talk to other influencers about your idea and seek their feedback and really refine your plan.

At this point, you've got a straw model of your community, which is intended to give you an image of what your building might look like, but isn't meant to stand the test of time. Go out and talk to people. Once you know whether your straw model is the design you want, you can start to build it in a way that is meant to last.

Pick three or four of the influencers with whom you have already connected. I suggest they be people you authentically respect and admire and who are within your reach. They might be more experienced or advanced than you, but they will likely pick up the phone when you call, engage with you and be willing to brainstorm your idea. They are the people you would want to have involved in creating your community. In other words, go to those whom you would pick as the leaders of your community and ask them for feedback.

They have likely run into similar ideas, either within your same target market or in other areas. They are probably going to be a wealth of advice and feedback.

One of the primary ways you can engage others is to paint a vision of what you want to create and to use your passion to enroll others in that vision.

When you are highly passionate, people are drawn to you. Influencers who are far more experienced and influential are likely to offer their support. Your vision and passion will easily enroll them. For a brief period of time, they're happy not to be leading, because in gifting you influence, they gain more influence of their own. They'll lead in the other areas that are more specific and relevant to their own business.

In essence, you paint a picture of how their world will be different because of this community that you're designing. Step into their world and their language to engage them and enroll them in the idea.

> **Unspoken Rule #14**
> *If you are not passionate about your vision of where you are going, don't expect people to follow.*

This homework is an exercise in practicing how well you can engage and enroll other influencers. You're going to be painting a vision that you're passionate about and seeing whether other influential people are willing to come along for the ride. If they're not, you can adjust and tweak the vision and then speak to other influencers about it. Do this a few times and you'll have the winning combination.

Mistake number one, the very first thing you learned in this book, was not aligning with your passion. This is a good point to check in. Did you design your community around something that you are really passionate about? If you didn't, it's going to become extremely challenging to start enrolling other influencers as you move forward.

Passion sells. People are drawn to fun. If you're not having a good time, you're no fun.

> *Passion sells. People are drawn to fun. If you're not having a good time, you're no fun.*

If you're not passionate enough to enroll the initial group of influencers you've chosen, you're going to have difficulty enrolling others as you expand your community. Check in and see whether you're really aligned and passionate about your goal. If you're not, that's not authentic for you.

Ensure you're not practicing at business. Did you pick a community that you thought would be successful, rather than one that you thought would really make a big impact on the area about which you're really passionate?

As you're receiving feedback, as you're seeing whether other influencers are engaging or becoming enrolled, you'll know whether or not you've hit the mark.

During the early stages of planning, you have the best opportunity to refine and change your plan. You've only spoken to a few people and they're certainly not going to think twice if you adjust and change, especially if you're doing so based on their feedback. It's likely that they're going to be flattered that you took their guidance and will be more enrolled.

Be prepared. You will likely receive conflicting advice or feedback and that's okay. Thank everyone for whatever feedback they give. Accepting feedback shows respect.

A common mistake you can make at this point is to assume you have to act on all the feedback that you receive. It's okay to collect feedback and decide which points to act on later. You don't have to use every piece of advice you receive. People want to know that they've been heard and they're just as likely to enroll in your idea later, whether or not you adjust based on their feedback.

Will the idea make money?

The next step is to look at whether the idea would make money. Advice from other influencers can be useful. Ultimately, you're in business to make money. It might not be the outcome or goal that you're targeting, but if you don't make money, you're not going to make a living at it. And then you're not in business. Money and influence can go hand in hand.

Who is going to join the community?

Think about who, specifically, you would invite to join this community. This is where you start to generate a list of potential names. You might have gotten some great advice from other influencers about this question. Some of them might have even offered to connect you with other appropriate people. Start keeping notes on possible members to invite and work that into your plan, because those initial contacts are going to become the heart and the founders of your community.

What logistics might be beneficial?

You have likely been given a lot of good ideas. Start making notes on the logistics you believe you want. For anything other than a mastermind, you're going to need a website, at a minimum. There may also be other systems you want to put in play to make your community work.

Determine the budget this would require

Do you want a website and conference lines? Where will you meet? What people might you contract or hire to pull this off?

What's the simplest or cheapest way to start your group?

It's a great idea initially to set it up based on something simple, because you're going to learn a lot from your trial runs and can adjust as you go.

How much of your time would be appropriate to build your community?

Consider designing it around the time that you have available. It's important to calculate how much time you have relative to the amount of time this community will require.

This is your chance to reassess. If you love the idea of your community, then either scale it to the time you have or find a way to create the time to do it.

At this point you should be able to create and take action on a complete plan including:

- ✓ whether you're creating a formal or informal community
- ✓ what type of community you want (mastermind, learning community, network, or a council)
- ✓ why you exist, the problem you solve for your industry and the problem you solve for the other influencers involved in your community
- ✓ the overall outcome
- ✓ how often you meet and how long
- ✓ who's involved
- ✓ who facilitates
- ✓ where you're meeting: online or off
- ✓ who you'll invite to the community
- ✓ a model for how to make money, if appropriate
- ✓ logistics, including budget
- ✓ a time budget - scaling the project to make it work for you.

CHAPTER 14
Taking Action, Living Your Dreams

"Living your dreams involves action. Otherwise you're just dreaming."
—Teresa de Grosbois

"I can't say I'm the biggest or the best marketer; I'm just a guy that just keeps doing it."

Dr. John Demartini is sitting across from me, matter-of-factly explaining how he's been blessed to be part of a group of thought leaders who have spearheaded one of the largest thought movements of the 20th and 21st centuries.

We're having lunch. At the age of 60 he's got a spring in his step, and looks like he's 45. I want to know his secret.

He's a world-renowned mindset expert and a pioneer in many respects. Many multi-millionaires have attributed their success to his work. In the industry he's also known as someone who generally does not do affiliate marketing, believing that if people appreciate, love and respect your work, they will refer you without being paid. I want to know how he got started, how he had the courage initially to buck the norm and try a whole new way of doing business that is radically different from what the rest of the industry is doing.

He modestly answers that he didn't even know he'd done that. And what comes next is so simple and so profound that it almost knocks me backward: "For 43 years I've just focused on contributing."

Influence is as simple and as difficult as that.

John doesn't think there's anything he has done that you couldn't also do for yourself. There's no magic formula. "I'm just a guy who's been researching every single day of my life for the last 43 years, trying to find solutions to different issues for humanity." And he continues to share the results of his research.

His dad told him when he was growing up, "If you deliver more than people expect, you'll never worry about business and rank," so he tries his best to keep delivering work that's mind-boggling, practical, useful and inspires people. "I've been told that if you stay with something long enough everyone else just dies out, and you'll get there."

I'm glued to my seat. The waitress is trying to get us to pay the bill and I don't want to miss a single word he says. I let my brief annoyance at the interruption pass. John continues:

I'm relentless in my research and relentless in my desire to give presentations. I just keep doing what I love most. I just keep delivering something I think will make a difference.

And if it doesn't work and serve, then the customer won't buy, so you have to find a balance between your narcissistic goal of trying to make a difference and your altruistic goal of trying to serve—playing the two together.

I've been on both sides of the pole where I've gone too far into myself and too far into others and I found that fair and equitable exchanges are the only things that actually last and work. You have to find something that serves others and which also serves you, otherwise it's not sustainable.

I've tried many things. Somehow, I've synchronously run into people who have helped me—all different types—and sometimes from places I least expected. Sometimes they're planned; but if it isn't fair and equitable, it doesn't sustain or work... you have to tweak it until it works, or you have to realize that just isn't the right match.

John is clear on the following point: "I research, write, travel and teach; that's it. I don't do the rest. I research every day. I write every day. I travel most days and I teach as much as I can daily."

John has become an expert at prioritizing, and lets his team do the rest: "If I get distracted by what I perceive to be low-priority things, I tend to get in my own way."

He goes on to stress that it's not that these things aren't important; they're low priority in his value system, and what is low priority for him is high priority to them. He has learned to go and do what he does best. He says he learned this from Mary Kay Ash of Mary Kay cosmetics nearly three decades ago. "I met Mary Kay and I asked her what advice she could give a young, aspiring, international speaker and she said, 'Everyday, write down the six or seven highest priority actions you can do that day that can help you fulfill your dream,' so on an index card I wrote them down every day and I did what she said and kept the cards. After a couple of years of doing that, I went back and reviewed all the cards and looked at what the highest priorities and four things rose to the top: research, write, travel and teach. So I said, 'Okay, I'm committed to delegating everything off my plate and I'm really going to do these four things,' and these four things have sustained me and I have also saved the hell out of my money. Whatever I earned, I saved half because I want my money working for me and not having to work for it all the time."

I know I've been leaning in the same direction. I now have a number of contractors and a team of volunteers working for me so I can delegate all the work I don't like doing and focus on where I'm really powerful. But when I look at my week, I can see more than 10 hours of rabbit holes

I've gone down. There is a level of greater intentionality I could have. I start taking stock.

I'm realizing the biggest gift of this meeting is that I'm sitting across from a man who epitomizes everything I teach. He is of high contribution to the world, is deeply passionate about what he does, he builds powerful relationships and, most importantly, he takes action, every day.

Habit #10: Influencers Take Action

There's a moment when you can see your results as a trainer. Invariably I come back to a city a few years after my last visit and see people who haven't seen me since I was last there. There's a moment when I see the results. I had two such moments recently.

The first moment is really sweet. A holistic nutritionist tells me how I've impacted her life. She tells me where she was a few years ago and how working through the week-to-week modules of my advanced course has shifted everything in how she works. She is now an internationally known best-selling author, making a lot more money and fully on fire. Her regret is not starting sooner, when we first met.

Exercise 17: The Two-Year Test

1. Write down your dream of what you'd like your life, or the world you live in, to become.

2. Note how far along that path you were two years ago vs. where you are today.

3. Compare the difference.

4. Make a note on your calendar to take the test again in two years.

I also have the second, less rewarding moment from someone who heard me speak two years ago. He liked my content then and likes it now. But somehow nothing has changed for him. He's still not ready to take action. All the same reasons are still in place—not enough time and resources to move forward.

The sad truth for most trainers is that we know some of you will love the content, walk away and never take a single action. You'll never implement the daily routine, never enroll in a single other training course. It's a lot like wanting to be a doctor and never going to medical school.

Although I've seen even the slowest of students achieve great results with consistent, committed action, the sad truth is that I more commonly see reasons for inaction.

The biggest difference between people who hold massive influence and those who don't isn't in the ideas they have or the plans they create, but in their choice to take action. Having the courage to move forward and take action on your plans is what sets you apart.

> **Unspoken Rule #15**
> *If you do not take some risk and put yourself out there, you will not be taken seriously by other influential people.*

No action, no results. So choose and move. It's the best gift you will ever give yourself.

Take action. Move forward with the plan you've just created. Remember, unspoken rule number two was, "I will not take you seriously if you play small when you deal with me. Have clarity, focus and confidence."

An adage you hear a lot in the entrepreneurial world is "Ready, fire, aim." Some of you will have misread that. Notice that I did not say "Ready, aim, fire". Seasoned entrepreneurs understand that sometimes you have to implement to see what your aim should have been. Sometimes you have to actually move forward and do something for a little while in order to understand whether it was the right target and the right fit.

Take a "ready, fire, aim" approach and give yourself permission to leap and then figure out whether the aim was perfect or not. It's easy to make small adjustments as you go. Give yourself permission to succeed sloppily.

COLUMBUS, LOOKING FOR A TRADE ROUTE TO INDIA, ACCIDENTALLY BUMPS INTO AMERICA.

Finding Your "Hell, Yes!" Plan

If you're still not a "hell, yes!" to the plan you created, think what it might take to change yourself to a firm, passionate yes. Sometimes it's just your internal game that needs to change. Make the decision and hold to it. If there are legitimately some external constraints, take the opportunity to look again at those constraints and figure out what support, infrastructure and resources you need to create success. You'll be far more effective at changing the world and impacting lives by stepping powerfully into the Influence Game.

Now that you've spoken to those first few key influencers, the next step is to develop a broader group of your founding members. The question to consider is how to enroll the broader group. Who do you want to be your active founding members, and how will you enroll those early adopters?

Celebrate Them

Celebrating your early supporters is key. The first people to come on board are the ones who actually create the community. You are not a leader until you have your first follower. Their role in creating your influence is pivotal.

You want to hold them in high esteem, and acknowledge them as highly influential within the group. Acknowledging your early adopters can include creating a charter member or founding member status, giving them a role as meeting facilitator or regional leader, or some other role or title to ensure they are celebrated within your group.

Think about whether or not you want to gift some kind of special status to those initial people to honor them. Treat them as leaders within the community, because they really are. They're the folks who jumped first. They're the folks who took action first. They are your core team. Special pricing, special status, any incentives you can think of, will solidify that initial group that will help you grow the community.

Once you've thought about what you're going to do with that initial group, think about how to encourage your first members to bring in other members. You have two clear options:

- Enrolling them in the vision of how a strong community is to their advantage. When that group is invested and able to come from a place of personal and community interest, they're going to be more motivated to bring in the right kinds of people who will strengthen the community.
- Consider an affiliate commission model or some kind of reward system for bringing in new members. There are pros and cons of using a commission model. The pro is it's very clear that you're thanking people for bringing in new members. The con is that it starts to shed doubt as to the motives for bringing new members in, because people start to worry that the money was main motivating factor.

By and large, the first option is always your strongest, but depending on your industry, you might want to use some combination of these ideas.

What If You Don't?

I can hear you through the pages of this book. You have your reasons to put this book down and say, "Great ideas, maybe someday I'll..."

If you never take a single action from this book, not much will change. Your life will stay pretty much as it is now—the good, the bad, the boring.

Some of you are just hard-wired for dealing with people one-on-one. You create change one life at a time and you simply know that's why you were put here. If that is you, I honor you, and the opportunities in this book may not call to you.

Some of you, however, know you were put here to do something bigger, to create change, to leave behind a world better than the one you came into. If you do not step into who you are, there will always be longing in your heart for something more - the ability to influence change.

But What If You Do?

I promise when you move forward on the actions in this book, it will at times be messy. Courage is never tidy. Consider a new way of thinking. Perhaps the highest state of perfection is learning to love the imperfect.

I also promise that your life will change. Living from a place of passion and doing something meaningful can bring joy and fulfillment to your life that makes everything richer and more meaningful. Think about what you are role modeling to your kids, friends and others in your life.

True influencers are dedicated, lifelong learners. Continue your training and expansion, because you were put here for a reason. You can influence a lot of conversations, a lot of growth in other people. This book has given you a good grounding in how to become a leader and influencer for change. Now it's your turn.

Living the life of your dreams requires action. Otherwise you're just dreaming. If you are ready, then step onto your path of influence.

YOU are the one the world is waiting for.

This is the start.

Resources and What's Next

For those of you who are leaping and are moving forward with implementing your action plan, there's a lot of information and learning beyond this book you might want to consider. Many of these resources are given on my website and mentioned in my bi-monthly newsletter at www.WildfireAcademy.com.

With the purchase of Mass Influence—the Habits of the Highly Influential you also received a complimentary tuition to The 30 Day Influence Challenge (worth $87).

This fun, engaging online training course supports the learning you will do in this book by having you complete 30 daily, 5-minute exercises. If you haven't already been, please visit www.MassInfluenceTheBook.com to sign up.

About the Authors

Teresa de Grosbois is an international speaker and three-time bestselling author hailing from Calgary, Canada. As an expert on influence, Teresa teaches courses around the globe on how to become an authority in your field and how to create word-of-mouth epidemics around your work. Teresa is the founder and chair of the Evolutionary Business Council, an international community of emerging thought leaders who focus on teaching the principles of success and prosperity.

Karen Rowe is a collaborative author, writing coach and book strategist living in Tampa, Florida. She turns business owners into authors and establishes them as experts in their industry. Karen is known for writing a book in three days and has ghostwritten books for some of the most fascinating people in the world, including a retired FBI Agent, a motion picture actor and a reality TV star.

References and Definitions

1. Cialdini, Robert B., *Influence: The Psychology of Persuasion,* Harper Business, 2006.

2. Gladwell, Malcolm, *The Tipping Point: How Little Things Can Make a Big Difference*, Little, Brown and Company, 2000.

3. Heath, Chip and Heath, Dan, *Made to Stick: Why Some Ideas Survive and Others Die*, Random House, 2007.

4. A gatekeeper in this context is a person that controls access to someone.

5. Source – Wikipedia.com - August 4, 2015

6. http://en.wikipedia.org/wiki/The_Huffington_Post - August 4, 2015

7. http://www.WellthLearning.com/ - August 4, 2015

8. Janet Bray Attwood and Chris Attwood, The Passion Test: The Effortless Path to Discovering Your Destiny, 1st World Publishing 2006.

9. http://www.mullychildrensfamily.org/ Note the spelling of The Mully Children's Family Charity has been altered to distinguish it from Charles Mulli the man. February 4, 2015

10. http://thewideawakening.com/

11. Sandberg, Sheryl, *Lean In: Women, Work, and the Will to Lead*, Knopf, 2013.

12. http://mymsuccess.com/ - March 8, 2015

13. Rogers, Everett, *Diffusion of Innovations,* 5th Edition. Simon & Schuster., 2003

14. www.thecoachingdept.com

15. R. A. Hill, & R. I. M. Dunbar, Social network size in humans, Human Nature, Volume 14, Issue 1, pp. 53-72., 2003

16. To tag someone use the @ sign before their name and it will automatically come up on their Facebook homepage.

17. Cycle of reciprocity is a term coined by Shawne Duperon in her networking and communications courses—her work on this topic is described in full in Chapter 10.

18. Bob Burg and John David Mann, *The Go-Giver: A Little Story About a Powerful Business Idea*, Portfolio, 2007.

99132117R00100

Made in the USA
Columbia, SC
05 July 2018